THE QUICK AFTER-WORK COOKBOOK

Here is the ideal cookbook for everyone who has to prepare a quick and nutritious meal after work, in an easy-to-follow style, Jill Cox includes

- delicious recipes for all the family to enjoy
- dishes for effortless but impressive entertaining
- a month's worth of healthy and different menus
- helpful larder lists to get you organised
- ideas for cakes you can make in a flash
- quick and interesting vegetarian meals
- invaluable hints, tips and shortcuts

The Quick After-Work Cookbook is the cookbook that everyone needs.

About the author

Jill Cox is a well-known food and wine writer and has written articles for numerous magazines and newspapers. She has regular columns in *TV Times*, *Hello!*, and *Decanter*, and has also appeared on radio and television.

Jill is the author of six other books, and lives in London.

THE
Quick
AFTER-WORK
COOKBOOK

Jill Cox

CORONET BOOKS
Hodder and Stoughton

Copyright © 1990 Jill Cox

First Published in Great Britain in 1990 by Judy Piatkus (Publishers) Limited

Coronet edition 1992
Second impression 1993

Designed by Paul Saunders
Illustrations by Mini Grey

The right of Jill Cox to be identified as the author of this work has been asserted by her in accordance with the Copyright, Designs and Patents Act 1988.

Printed and bound in Great Britain for Hodder and Stoughton Paperbacks, a division of Hodder and Stoughton Ltd., Mill Road, Dunton Green, Sevenoaks, Kent TN13 2YA (Editorial Office: 47 Bedford Square, London WC1B 3DP) by Clays Ltd, St Ives plc.

British Library C.I.P.

A CIP catalogue record for this title is available from the British Library

ISBN 0-340-564539

CONTENTS

———◇———

ACKNOWLEDGEMENTS

The author's special thanks go to Alison Grainge and Dianne Curtin.

And the publishers would like to thank the following organisations for supplying the photographs used in this book:

British Meat (opposite pages 32 and 33)
Pasta Information Centre (opposite pages 64 and 129)
Scottish Salmon Information Service (opposite page 65)
Modern Health Products Ltd (opposite page 128)

INTRODUCTION

————◇————

The trouble with the working day is that most of the time is taken up with getting to the work place, doing the job and coming home again. Even if you're a busy mum who is tied to the home, when in all honesty do you even have time to think seriously about the catering?

And if you do work away from home what is the first thing you do after you've crawled back? Any remaining energy gets used making a cup of tea or pouring a huge gin and tonic. So it's little surprise that many working people quite frequently opt for eating out, or dialling for a takeaway – preferably from a firm which delivers.

Anyone who has the time to think about an evening meal during a frantic lunchtime will more than likely grab a ready-prepared meal or something fast and frozen. And who can blame them? Many such items are quality products that taste great. You can even get away with using them for a dinner party with only the teeniest disguise.

But, on the other hand, they can cost a prince's ransom. And if you are a long-suffering working parent with huge appetites to satisfy, it quickly becomes obvious that to cut out cooking means you need at least *two* jobs – just to pay the food bills.

Apart from this, you feel guilty. And, say what you like, you eventually get bored with pre-packed food and takeaway meals. Anyone who is remotely keen on eating has an (admittedly often quite cleverly hidden) urge to produce interesting, appetising and nourishing food. If you are a parent it's practically obligatory to do so – it shows you care!

This book is your salvation. It will induce peace of mind and confidence in the busy, racing-against-time cook who has to prepare a meal every day. It also takes the strain off special occasion cookery. It's packed with tried and tested recipes and time-saving, labour-saving, reputation-making suggestions and tips, all designed to lighten the load of the harassed after-work cook.

7

GETTING ORGANISED

———◇———

Organisation should be the key word in the vocabulary of any working person. But however brilliantly efficient you may be at your job, you'd have to be superhuman to run your home on the same lines – at least as far as the shopping and cooking are concerned. Some of us are superhuman, of course, but let's face it, most of us are not.

A certain degree of organisation is necessary if you don't want to find yourself gazing into the fridge, wondering what you could possibly do with one beefburger, six egg whites and eight cooked sprouts. What you need are menus and storecupboard lists. And who is going to think up delicious, interesting and varied menus, you ask? More about this later. First you need to look at what's on the shelves in your larder, fridge and freezer. And then be ruthless.

STORECUPBOARD LISTS

The following lists contain items that are a) needed all the time and b) to be kept handy in case of emergency, or when you invite people on the spur of the moment for something to eat.

The Larder

Larders are their own worst enemies. All those shelves just crying out for something to be put on them. And when they've been filled up, what do you do? Squeeze even more things in sideways, on top, so you can't even read what they are. Things like jellies, cake mixes and tins of mushy peas will still be there this time next year. Most of the time you only ever use the last item in.

It's an inbuilt instinct to provide for a famine or an unforeseen shortage. But you would need to be very near death from starvation to chew your way through the contents of a split pack of leathery dried figs and a couple of dozen concrete stock cubes. So chuck them all out and start again.

Always
Canned fish
Tuna, sardines, anchovies, pilchards

Vegetables
Canned tomatoes (chopped are useful if a bit more expensive), tomato purée, instant mash, canned new potatoes, canned sweetcorn

Fruit
Canned: pineapple, apricots, peaches, figs, stoned black cherries
Dried: sultanas, seedless raisins, dates, apricots, prunes, glacé cherries

Nuts
Flaked almonds, ground almonds, walnuts, peanuts

Pulses
Canned: chickpeas, red kidney beans, haricot beans, baked beans
Dried: lentils, chickpeas, red kidney beans

Rice
Easy-cook long grain rice, pudding rice, canned cooked rice

Pasta
Tagliatelle, macaroni, packet of pasta shapes, egg noodles

Flour and cereals
Plain and self raising flour, wholemeal flour, cornflour
Packets of breakfast cereal, muesli, oats

Sugar and syrup
Caster sugar, icing sugar, brown sugar, golden syrup

Dried herbs
Bouquet garni, thyme, basil, dill, rosemary, tarragon, bay leaves, oregano

Spices
Black and white peppercorns, paprika, cayenne, chilli powder, ground cinnamon, cinnamon sticks, ground coriander, caraway

seeds, sesame seeds, whole nutmeg, cloves, ground ginger, root ginger, vanilla essence

Oils
Sunflower oil, olive oil

Vinegars
White and red wine vinegar

Sauces and flavourings
Pasta sauces, pour-over sauces, cook-in sauces, canned custard
English mustard powder, Dijon mustard, wholegrain mustard
Anchovy essence, soy sauce, tabasco sauce, Worcestershire sauce, tomato sauce, lemon juice

Stock cubes or concentrates
All types including vegetable and fish

Relishes and preserves
Mango chutney, piccallili
Jams, honey

Drinks
Instant coffee, ground coffee, teas, cocoa powder, coffee essence

Miscellaneous
Plain chocolate bars, flan cases, *langue de chat* and ratafias or other dessert biscuits

Sometimes
Canned fish
Salmon, crab, mussels

Vegetables
Canned: petit pois, artichoke hearts, asparagus, palm hearts

Fruit
Canned: lychees, mangoes
Bottled: fruit sauce

Nuts
Pine nuts, desiccated coconut

Pulses
Canned: flageolet beans
Dried: butter beans

Oils
Walnut oil, hazelnut oil, sesame oil

Vinegars
Tarragon vinegar, raspberry vinegar, sherry vinegar

Sauces and flavourings
Mushroom ketchup

Relishes and preserves
Maple syrup

The fridge

The sensible working person chooses a small fridge which fits under a worktop. There is logic in this: a) there is not *too* much space to fill up which ensures a reasonable turnover and b) you will use it for what it was designed – keeping food chilled so it doesn't go off – and not as an extension of the larder. (Although these days products which are preservative-free *have* to be kept in the fridge instead of the larder.)

Always
Milk, cream and/or natural yogurt, eggs, butter, cheese, margarine

Salad ingredients, a made-up jar of vinaigrette, opened jar of mayonnaise and other opened products which are preservative-free

Orange juice, bottled water

Sometimes
White or rosé wine

Ready-prepared chilled meals

The freezer

The working person who scarcely has time to live certainly has no free hours to cook simply to fill the freezer with ready-made dishes. Even though these days the microwave provides the fast way to bring frozen dishes to the table, no busy person cooks for the freezer any more.

But it is a prudent provider who keeps a few pizzas, boeufs à la bourguignonne, ice cream, frozen chicken pieces, fish fillets, fish fingers and a clutch of frozen vegetables in a small-to-medium-size freezer, ready to flash to the table with the flourish of someone who has spent several hours slaving over a hot stove.

Should you be so organised a cook that you do start preparing in advance, it's very useful to be able to make and store the goulash the week before it's needed to take the grind out of the work on the day. Or make double quantities when you do cook and store half for use later.

Regard your freezer as a sophisticated cupboard in which to keep bought frozen food that, once thawed and possibly tinkered with, would pass for fresh. The name of the game is to cheat and not be found out!

Always
Puff and shortcrust pastry

Fish, shelled prawns, fish fingers

Minced beef, beef burgers, a chicken, chicken pieces, chicken stock, leg of lamb, bacon, sausages

Oven chips, peas, green beans, spinach, herbs

Bread and breadcrumbs

Butter

Stir-fries, pizzas and any frozen prepared dishes which you specially like or which will please unexpected guests, like chicken Kiev

Raspberries, gâteaux, ice cream

SHOPPING

There are those who favour the once-a-week supermarket shop. This has its advantages. It may well work out cheaper – certainly in terms of travelling expenses – and you won't need to go shopping again that week. But on the other hand, supermarkets are a den of temptation and unless you plan and stick firmly to your list you'll buy things you don't really need.

If you shop daily it's easier to be disciplined but unless you're the kind of person who can plan a meal while on your feet, you'll more than likely end up with random purchases and no real idea of what to do with them. If you shop in your lunch hour you'll have the added problem of where to store the food at work. If there isn't a fridge you'll only be able to buy items that don't need refrigerating – meat and fish etc will have to be bought at other times.

So menu planning and shopping with a strict list relating to this are essential to prudent purchasing. However, planning is time-consuming, which is why this book has an extremely useful section – 'A Month of Menus'. Once you've chosen a menu, check the ingredients list for each dish. What you don't have in the storecupboard, fridge or freezer, put on your shopping list.

EQUIPMENT

There are nowadays so many highly specialised kitchen gadgets available that it's difficult to know which are essential. Who hasn't used up a whole bag of potatoes trying out the latest kind of lethally-bladed, razor-sharp mandolin? Or juiced every last apple and carrot in the house justifying how essential it was to own the latest attachment to the food processor?

Assuming that you have all the basics (bowls, pans, measuring jug, pastry brush, baking beans, kebab skewers, etc), what 'extras' do you really need?

Food processor
A decent sized food processor is like two extra pairs of hands and certainly worth the investment. Not only will it slice, shred, chop and mix, but it will also make cakes and pastry. OK, the working cook buys these whenever possible, but sometimes you *have* to make them yourself. Incidentally, don't waste time washing up the bowl between functions if they are all part of the same recipe. Work out the most sensible order to process the ingredients in before you begin (e.g. chop dry ingredients before processing a wet mixture).

Electric whisk
An electric whisk beats and whips much more quickly than the old fashioned rotary whisk. The hand held type can be used in any bowl that's big enough, and even in a saucepan, which can save on washing up.

Slow cooker

If you are out at work, a slow cooker is a good chum too, though you can get the same effect by cooking stews and casseroles all day at 225°F/110°C/Gas ¼ in your trusty cooker, so long as it is in a pot with a well-fitting lid. This of course needs advance thought and preparation.

Pressure cooker

The pressure cooker is a great asset in any kitchen. Vegetables are cooked in minutes, even potatoes; and the toughest old meat becomes meltingly tender in its own delicious gravy with the help of one of these. Sometimes the pressure cooker can be even quicker than the lightning kitchen aid – the microwave.

Microwave oven

The latest type of microwave combines a convection oven facility, a grill, and just about anything else they didn't have before – plus computerised touch-sensitive controls which work out the details of cooking times for you. A microwave and convection oven together can cope more than adequately with probably 50 per cent of cooking requirements. Plus they do a load of jobs the conventional cooker can't. And in this day and age when the average family does not always sit down together to eat, and we do occasionally buy ready-prepared or frozen dishes for convenience, then a method of thawing and heating which does not destroy the food or remove all the nutrients is very useful – even if all you're doing is giving the fish and chips a quick blast! There are some recipes for speedy microwave dishes on pages 131–40.

Wok

Stir-frying is a very quick and healthy way to cook. Best results are achieved in a wok – a large dish-shaped pan with a rounded bottom. They can also be used for deep-frying, steaming and braising.

Dishwasher

Nobody likes doing the washing-up, and after a hard day's work followed by cooking a meal, it's the last thing you'll want to do. If the rest of the family are less than helpful, a dishwasher may be the answer – if you have the space.

Miscellaneous

Quirky moulds, chocolate pots, lasagne dishes, sweetcorn or avocado dishes, oyster plates, ravioli mats, biscuit rolling pins, meat thermometers, pasta and yogurt makers, asparagus steamers, fondue pots – well, these are your own affair.

BASIC RECIPES AND SHORT CUTS

There are certain basic food items that the busy cook shouldn't even attempt to make, like puff and shortcrust pastry. This is not only because they are time-consuming, but because the ready-prepared versions are reliable and readily available. However other essentials, like vinaigrette, are so quickly and easily made that to pay the inflated prices for the ready-made variety really is a waste of money.

Pastry

Shortcrust pastry

Buy it. There is no need to even waste the 10 minutes it takes to make. Especially if you have hot hands and the pastry is likely to be tough and leathery. It is available both plain and wholemeal.

Keep frozen pastry in the freezer *always* – you never know when you might need it. Defrost conventionally at room temperature for 30 minutes–1 hour or in the fridge overnight. Avoid thawing it in the microwave as the pastry can start cooking around the edges.

When making pastry cases it is best to chill them before cooking, whether you are putting the filling in straight away or baking the cases blind (see below). This should be for at least 15 minutes, but you can reduce this if you're really pushed for time and don't mind the possibility of an uneven tart. In this case, chill for 7 minutes then brush the pastry with egg white before baking blind. Usually there will be enough egg white left inside the shell of an egg used in the filling to avoid cracking another.

Baking blind

For best results, shortcrust pastry cases should be baked blind. After chilling, prick the base all over with a fork, cover with greaseproof paper and fill with baking beans. Bake at 400°F/200°C/Gas 6 for 7 minutes. The pastry case can then be filled and baked according to the recipe.

Puff pastry

Nobody in their right minds will attempt to make puff pastry if they are aiming for quick and easy results. Instead buy it ready-made. If you buy it frozen, thaw it slowly, preferably in the fridge. Frozen ready-to-bake vol au vent cases can be cooked from frozen. Follow the instructions on the packet.

Ready-made pastry cases

Ready-made pre-cooked pastry cases are the busy cook's salvation, as no time is lost rolling out or lining tins. They are available savoury or sweet, and plain or wholemeal in a variety of sizes.

Stocks

Busy cooks simply don't need to spend time making beef, fish or vegetable stock when there are so many reliable stock cubes, powders and concentrates available – additive and salt-free for an authentic flavour. Canned consommé can even take the place of meat stock and for instant vegetable stock, simply use the cooking water from vegetables, especially green ones.

Chicken stock

Making chicken stock, however, is a different matter. Boiling up a poultry carcase may sound like yet another thankless task to set before the already strapped-for-time cook, but in fact it's not. It really *does* make a delicious stock or soup that's worth every second it takes. And most of that time is spent simmering, which requires little or no supervision.

Simply cram the chicken bones into your largest saucepan, add any leftover vegetables, a whole onion (the skin gives the stock a good golden colour) and a carrot or two, and cover with water. Bring to the boil then turn down the heat, cover and leave to simmer for an hour. Strain, cool, then skim off any fat. You can speed up the cooking with a pressure cooker.

Use the stock as it is in sauces and soups, or reduce until it tastes strong enough, season to taste and serve as delicious homemade chicken soup.

Home-made stock freezes well. Either freeze in a large container, or reduce the stock and freeze in ice cube trays. Transfer the cubes to freezer bags once they are frozen. Drop the cubes into gravy and sauces to make them extra tasty.

Frozen stock can be used straight from the freezer. Melt in a saucepan over a low heat then bring to the boil and boil for two minutes.

To Stabilise Yogurt

In this health-conscious age people are turning away from using cream in their cooking, and restricting its use to special occasions. The odd splash of cream in sauces and desserts turns them into something a little more luxurious. However in the recipes in this book alternatives are suggested where applicable, such as yogurt.

When using yogurt in cooking, it needs to be stabilised first to prevent it separating. Whether it's healthy low-fat yogurt or the more creamy Greek yogurt, mix it with flour before adding to a hot sauce or dish. Use 1 tablespoon flour for each ¼ pint/150ml yogurt.

Dressings and Sauces

Big, chunky salads can often be a complete meal in themselves while the more delicate ones make a delicious accompaniment to cold and hot dishes alike.

But no salad is happy without a dressing. Substantial salads like potato- and pasta-based ones are best with a creamy sauce based on mayonnaise, soured cream or yogurt. Crisp leaves and slivered vegetables, on the other hand, are more suited to the lightest brush of a thinner dressing – like a vinaigrette.

Here are a few basic and not so basic ideas for dressings.

Vinaigrette
—◇—

This is the most useful dressing for all kinds of salads. Use it as a base and *do* vary it – oil-wise, vinegar-wise, seasoning-wise (see suggestions below) – just taste to see if you like it. It's a good idea to make a large batch of the basic vinaigrette at the start of the week which can then be flavoured as required. Make it in the proportions of 4 parts oil to 1 part vinegar.

> *4 tbsp sunflower oil*
> *1 tbsp white wine vinegar*
> *1 tsp Dijon mustard*
> *squeeze of lemon juice*
> *salt and freshly ground black pepper*

Shake all the ingredients together in a screw-top jar and keep in the fridge ready for use. Shake well before pouring over a salad.

Variations Add the following ingredients to the above quantity of basic vinaigrette.

Lemon, Orange or Lime Vinaigrette
Zest and juice of half a lemon or orange or of a whole lime.

Herb Vinaigrette
One tablespoon of chopped herbs such as basil, chives or tarragon.

Spicy Vinaigrette
One dried red chilli, finely shredded. Leave to marinate overnight.

Garlic Vinaigrette
Two cloves of garlic, peeled and crushed, and a finely sliced spring onion.

Mustard Vinaigrette
Substitute wholegrain mustard for the Dijon.

Raspberry Vinaigrette
Substitute raspberry vinegar for white wine vinegar.

Hazelnut or Walnut Vinaigrette
Substitute hazelnut or walnut oil for sunflower oil.

Mayonnaise

———◇———

Busy cooks will use bought mayonnaise most of the time, but home-made tastes so great that everyone should know how to make it — even if only for special occasions.

Makes ½ pint/300 ml

2 egg yolks
2 tsp made mustard
good squeeze lemon juice
salt and freshly ground white pepper
½ pt/300ml sunflower oil

Put yolks, mustard, lemon juice, salt and white pepper in a bowl and blend with an electric beater. Gradually add oil drip by drip until the mixture begins to thicken. Then add the oil in a thin stream, beating all the time, making sure each addition is incorporated before adding any more.

Variations Add the following ingredients to each ½ pt/300 ml home-made or bought mayonnaise.

Curried Mayonnaise
Two teaspoons of curry paste, or to taste.

Tomato Mayonnaise
Two teaspoons of tomato purée.

Garlic Mayonnaise
Three cloves of garlic, peeled and crushed.

Herb Mayonnaise
One teaspoon of freshly chopped fresh herbs.

Tartare Sauce
One teaspoon of chopped capers and gherkins.

Soured Cream Dressing
———◇———

This is lighter and less calorie-laden than mayonnaise on its own. Simply mix together equal quantities of mayonnaise and soured cream.

For a variation add 2 teaspoons of lemon juice, 1 teaspoon of grated onion and salt and white pepper to taste to each ½ pint/300 ml Soured Cream Dressing.

Substitute low fat yogurt for the soured cream to make an even healthier dressing.

Tomato Sauce
———◇———

A quick and tasty tomato sauce, good with fish cakes, pasta or burgers.

Serves 4

Total time: 10–15 minutes

1 tbsp oil
1 small onion, peeled and finely chopped
1 clove garlic, peeled and crushed
14oz/400g can chopped tomatoes
1 level tsp dried basil
salt and freshly ground black pepper

Heat oil in a pan and fry onion and garlic until soft. Add tomatoes and juice and mash down well. Add the basil then increase the heat and continue cooking until the mixture has thickened.

Season with salt and pepper. Purée for a smooth sauce or leave chunky.

A MONTH OF MENUS

———◇———

'What shall we have for supper tonight?' This dreaded question faces all after-work cooks every day of the week. The answer doesn't come in one word, as choosing the main dish is only the beginning – there is what to serve *with* and *after* or *before* it to consider as well.

A menu requires a little forethought. A hefty main course needs a light dessert and a rich pud should only follow a simple meal. Textures and colours are important too. Try to keep a balance of crunch and cream. And don't go overboard on colour schemes. On the other hand, don't go to the opposite extreme and serve, say poached chicken breasts in a cream sauce with rice, on a white plate, followed by lychees in a white bowl! There's no stimulation for the eye here, and visual presentation is almost as important as the cooking itself.

Subtle garnish can make all the difference in the world to what seems a very simple dish. Arrange grilled chops or fish on lots of watercress – in fact any leaves will do, from crinkly savoys to raw spinach or celery tops. Lemon, lime or orange wedges or slices are effective on both sweet and savoury dishes; chopped fresh herbs make vegetables look pretty, and sliced almonds will dress up and add texture to many a salad or pud.

The following menus have been planned with all this advice in mind. They are mostly two-course meals, as they are intended for days when simplicity, cost and speed are paramount. But add an idea of your own if you think you'll go hungry after only two courses. Or you could always offer a little cheese to finish.

Salad accompaniments feature quite largely in the menus. They are not only healthy but generally save on washing up too. Substitute a seasonal hot vegetable if you prefer.

These recipes aren't the quickest in the world – plain grilled lamb chops would be quicker to prepare than the Marinated Lamb with Garlic and Rosemary from the first menu. But which is the tastier?

Here are new suggestions for interesting speedy meals, as well as quicker ways to create old favourites, all incorporating modern ingredients and shortcuts. The Cook's Tips boxes provide yet more short cuts as well as suggesting alternative ingredients.

There is an emphasis on dishes using pasta and fillets of meat, poultry and fish because these items are quick-to-cook.

There are 31 menus – one for every day of the month. They are designed to help you plan but you can swap dishes about depending on what is available – and on what you have in the fridge or larder. You can simply run through the menus from 1 to 31, or jump around and make them in any order you fancy.

At the beginning of each menu is a brief guide to the order of preparation for that meal. To help you even more, the total time each menu takes to prepare and cook is given. The maximum time taken is 1 hour 10 minutes, but even that doesn't mean an hour's solid work in the kitchen – it's simply that one of the dishes requires longer cooking in the oven. If any part of the menu has to be made in advance it is indicated here.

All the menus serve **four**.

A BRIEF GUIDE TO WINE

The trend these days seems to be to pick up a bottle of wine when you're shopping in the supermarket. In terms of quality, you won't go far wrong if you do this. Supermarkets employ highly qualified buyers who seek out excellent wines. Their immense buying power means that they can offer the wines at bargain prices, which are often much lower than those of an independent shop selling the same wines.

What to drink with what is a problem which ought not to exist. Whilst some combinations of wine and food are better than others, there are no hard and fast rules. The 'red wine with red meat and white wine with fish' idea is a mere guideline. You drink what you like with whatever you choose. It's up to you.

Obviously there is not a lot of sense in spending much on a bottle of wine to drink with a fiery curry – you wouldn't be able to taste the wine. And a dish with a sharp or lemony sauce will wreck the taste of wine too. But this is simply commonsense.

Aside from this, the most important thing to consider is – do you like it?

Most people begin with something white, scented, low in alcohol and with a medium-sweet taste. The German Liebfraumilch is still the supermarket's best seller. It's cheap, and easy to drink – the only problem is the long German name!

When choosing wines you will generally find shelf-notes to guide you – but remember, they are only a guide. Let wine drinking be the exciting adventure you want it to be.

Here's a rule-of-thumb guide for beginners, which you can change to suit yourself:

Fish
Dry white wine from the Loire in France; Sauvignon Blanc from New Zealand; Macon from Burgundy.

Chicken
Chardonnay from Australia or New Zealand; white Rhone; white new-style Rioja; Vouvray from the Loire; Beaujolais; Valpolicella.

Beef
Burgundy; reds from the Southern Rhone, Australian Shiraz; red Rioja: Chianti Classico.

Lamb
Bordeaux; Chianti; red Rioja.

Vegetarian food
Frascati from Italy; Chinon from the Loire; English wine; Sauvignon Blanc.

MENU 1

—◇—

Marinated Lamb with Garlic and Rosemary
French Beans
Rosti

Zappy Zabaglione

A meal with a continental flavour.

Marinate the lamb first. Then make the Zappy Zabaglione and leave to chill in the fridge. Next make the Rosti and start frying the lamb steaks just before you turn the Rosti over to cook on the second side. You will need 2 frying pans.

Total time: 45 minutes

Marinated Lamb with Garlic and Rosemary

—◇—

The new cuts of lamb include leg steaks, which make very fast midweek suppers. They are tender and particularly delicious when cooked with garlic and rosemary.

2 tbsp finely chopped fresh parsley
1 tsp chopped fresh rosemary
grated zest of 1 lemon
4 cloves garlic, crushed
4 lamb leg steaks
salt and freshly ground black pepper
1oz/25g butter
2 tbsp oil
lemon wedges to decorate

Mix together parsley, rosemary, lemon zest and garlic in a bowl. Pat mixture on to both sides of each steak and leave to marinate for 30 minutes.

Season steaks with salt and pepper. Heat butter and oil in a pan and fry steaks for 6 minutes each side or until cooked to your liking. Serve immediately with pan juices poured over and garnished with lemon wedges, accompanied by French beans and Rosti.

Rosti
————◇————

This is a Swiss potato dish that you serve in wedges like a cake. It's something different to do with potatoes!

2lb/900g potatoes, scrubbed
1 onion, peeled and grated
salt and freshly ground black pepper
1 tbsp oil
1oz/25g butter

Par-boil potatoes in plenty of lightly salted boiling water for about 7 minutes. Drain and cool slightly.

Peel and grate the potatoes into a bowl. You can leave the peel on if you prefer. Add grated onion and mix well. Season with salt and pepper.

With lightly floured hands, form potato mixture into a large flat cake. Heat oil and butter in a pan and fry potato cake gently for about 10 minutes until the underside is brown. Gently flip the cake over and fry on the other side. (See Cook's Tips on page 26 for a fail-safe method of turning the Rosti over.) Serve cut into wedges.

Zappy Zabaglione

———◇———

A rich and creamy no-cook Zabaglione.

4 egg yolks
2 tbsp caster sugar
2 tbsp marsala or sweet sherry
Lemon curls to decorate (see Cook's Tips)

Whisk all the ingredients together with an electric beater until light, thick and creamy. Pour into wine glasses and chill for 30 minutes. Decorate with lemon curls just before serving.

Cook's Tips

———◇———

- Use ½ tsp dried rosemary on the lamb leg steaks, if you don't have fresh rosemary. As a general rule, if replacing fresh herbs with dried, halve the quantity – or add to taste.
- Waxy potatoes make the best Rosti. Varieties to use include Cyprus and Maris Piper. To turn the Rosti over, place a large flat plate over the saucepan and hold in place while you turn the pan upside down. The potato cake will now be on the plate. Set the frying pan back on the heat and carefully slide the cake off the plate and into the pan.
- To make lemon curls to decorate the pud, carefully pare thin curls of zest from the outside of a washed lemon. You can make the Zappy Zabaglione with a hand whisk instead of an electric beater, but it will take longer.

MENU 2

————◇————

Dijon Chicken
Green Rice with Almonds

Apricot Fool

This is quite a sophisticated but simple-to-prepare menu.

Make the fool first so it has time to chill in the fridge while you prepare the chicken and rice.

Total time: 40 minutes

Dijon Chicken

————◇————

Skinned, boned chicken breasts, found in most supermarkets, provide the basis for lots of fast dishes.

1 tbsp oil
½ onion, peeled and chopped
1 clove garlic, peeled and crushed
4 skinless chicken breast fillets, cut into strips
3 tsp Dijon mustard
4 tbsp orange juice
½ tsp chopped fresh dill
salt and freshly ground black pepper
¼ pint/150ml soured cream

Heat oil in a pan and cook onion and garlic until soft, but not brown.
Add chicken to pan and cook until stiffened, turning once or twice.
Add mustard, orange juice and dill. Reduce heat, cover and simmer for about 5 minutes or until the chicken is cooked through. Season with salt and pepper. Stir through the soured cream and gently reheat before serving.

27

Green Rice with Almonds

---◇---

Everyone has their own idea of how to cook rice. This is one way that is pretty fool proof. After cooking and draining the rice return it to the pan and push a clean teatowel down into the pan to cover the rice. This acts as a lid, as well as absorbing any excess moisture and results in perfect, separate grains. It will also keep the rice hot for quite a long time if you find your other preparations are taking extra time.

8oz/225g easy-cook long grain rice
1oz/25g butter
1 bunch spring onions, trimmed and finely chopped
2 tbsp finely chopped fresh parsley
salt and freshly ground black pepper
1 tbsp flaked almonds, toasted (see Cook's Tips)

Plunge rice into a large pan of boiling salted water and simmer for exactly 14 minutes. Remove from heat, drain, then return to pan.

Push a clean teatowel into the saucepan to cover the rice and leave to finish itself off in the steam for about 5 minutes. Leave the lid off the saucepan.

Remove the teatowel and stir butter through the hot rice, then mix in the onions and parsley. Season with salt and pepper and sprinkle over almonds to serve.

Apricot Fool
—◇—

A delicate topaz pudding made in a flash.

14oz/400g can apricots in natural juice, drained
8oz/225g Greek yogurt
langue de chat *or* flute *biscuits, to serve*

Purée the fruit in a blender or food processor then stir in the yogurt.
Pour into 4 individual serving dishes and chill for at least 30 minutes.
Serve with biscuits.

Cook's Tips
—◇—

- No soured cream for the Dijon chicken? Sour a little left-over double cream by adding a squeeze of lemon juice or use stabilised yogurt instead (see page 17).
- Chop parsley with a sharp knife for best results. A food processor can make it too wet and isn't much quicker as you then have the bowl to wash up.
- Open freeze parsley sprigs then pack in freezer bags. They can be crumbled straight from the freezer – there's no need to chop them.
- For extra speed use canned cooked rice to make the Green Rice with Almonds.
- To toast almonds, place under the grill on a piece of foil. Use gentle heat to avoid scorching them.
- A summer fruit fool can be made by substituting fresh seasonal berries and soft fruit for the canned apricots.

MENU 3

—◇—

Finny Hinn
Tomato and Green Bean Salad

Citrus Spritz

A fresh-tasting light meal with a lovely mix of flavours.

Prepare the quiche first. While it's cooking make the Citrus Spritz and leave to chill in the fridge. Then make the Tomato and Green Bean Salad.

Total time: 1 hour

Finny Hinn

—◇—

This is a smoked haddock and sweetcorn quiche. It is sunshine yellow and has an interesting texture. You can use canned or frozen sweetcorn, as long as it is thawed and/or well drained first.

6oz/175g shortcrust pastry
6oz/175g smoked haddock
¼ pint/150ml milk
4oz/100g sweetcorn kernels, drained
2oz/50g Cheddar cheese, grated
3 eggs
¼ pint/150ml single cream
salt and freshly ground black pepper

Lightly grease a 9 inch/23 cm flan tin. Roll out pastry on a lightly floured board and line tin. Chill for 15 minutes.

Preheat oven to 375°F/190°C/Gas 5.

Meanwhile, place haddock in a pan and pour over milk. Poach for

10 minutes, or until cooked through. Drain fish and reserve poaching liquid. Allow to cool slightly then skin fish, remove any bones, and flake.

Scatter fish flakes over pastry case and sprinkle over sweetcorn and cheese. Beat eggs with cream and reserved cooking liquid then season with salt and pepper. Pour into flan case. Bake for 45 minutes or until set.

Tomato and Green Bean Salad

———◇———

This red and green salad makes a stunning contrast to the sunshine yellow quiche.

8oz/225g green beans, topped and tailed
8oz/225g tomatoes, quartered
½ small onion, peeled and finely chopped
1 tbsp finely chopped fresh parsley
1 quantity Vinaigrette (see page 18)

Cook beans in plenty of boiling salted water for 4 minutes. Drain and plunge into cold water. Drain again.

Mix beans with tomatoes in a serving bowl. Sprinkle over onion and parsley. Pour Vinaigrette over salad just before serving.

Citrus Spritz
— ◇ —

A juicy and refreshing salad of grapefruit and mint. It provides an unexpected end to the meal and complements the main course well.

2 large grapefruit, peeled and cut into segments
2 tbsp mint syrup (see Cook's Tips)
2 tbsp vodka or fruit juice
1 tbsp finely chopped fresh mint
mint sprig for decoration

Place grapefruit segments in a shallow serving dish. Pour over mint syrup and vodka or fruit juice. Stir, then leave to infuse for at least half an hour in the fridge.

Stir through chopped mint just before serving and decorate with a whole mint sprig.

Cook's Tips
— ◇ —

- Grate hard leftover knobs of cheese and keep covered in the fridge ready to use.
- Fresh green beans are best for the salad – but you could use frozen instead.
- Make sure you remove all the pith from the grapefruit segments when preparing the pud. Use a serrated knife.
- If you prefer, use gin or fruit juice instead of the vodka in the Citrus Spritz.
- Mint syrup is readily available in supermarkets and delicatessens. It's a concentrated syrup that is diluted to make drinks.

MENU 4

———◇———

Aegean Aubergines
Red Cabbage and Apple Salad

Crazy Crumble

A cheap and cheerful midweek meal.

Prepare the salad while the aubergines are baking, but don't dress it until just before serving. Bake the crazy crumble alongside the aubergines.

Total time: 45 minutes

Aegean Aubergines

———◇———

These are aubergines stuffed with a mixture of chicken livers and mushrooms. For the best flavour choose firm, glossy aubergines.

2 large aubergines
2oz/50g butter
1 onion, peeled and finely chopped
1lb/450g chicken livers, trimmed, washed and dried
½lb/225g button mushrooms, wiped and sliced
2 tomatoes, skinned and chopped
pinch dried oregano
salt and freshly ground black pepper

Preheat oven to 350°F/180°C/Gas 4.

Score a line around the aubergines lengthwise. Place on a greased baking tray and bake for 25 minutes or until soft. Remove from oven and increase heat to 400°F/200°C/Gas 6.

Carefully cut each aubergine in half and scoop the flesh on to a board. Chop the flesh and reserve the shells.

Melt butter in a pan and gently fry onion for 2 minutes until soft. Turn up heat and add chicken livers. Fry quickly, turning until browned all over. Add mushrooms and cook for a further 2 minutes.

Stir in tomatoes and oregano and chopped aubergine flesh. Season with salt and pepper. Pile mixture into aubergine shells, return to the baking tray and bake for 10 minutes.

Red Cabbage and Apple Salad
—◇—

A colourful and crunchy salad.

1 crisp green apple
lemon juice
1lb/450g red cabbage, cored and shredded
½ Spanish onion, peeled and finely chopped
4 tbsp Vinaigrette (see page 18)

Core the apple and cut into chunks. Sprinkle over lemon juice. Put cabbage, apple and onion in a large bowl. Drizzle over the Vinaigrette and toss gently.

Crazy Crumble
———◊———

A fast and spectacularly simple crumble, using leftover sponge cake.
Even a child can make this!

2 x 14oz/400g cans mixed red fruits
8oz/225g leftover sponge cake
2 tbsp ground almonds
1 tbsp demerara sugar
cream or custard, to serve

Preheat oven to 400°F/200°C/Gas 6.
    Pour fruit into the base of an ovenproof glass dish. Crumble cake
in a food processor or with the fingers. Mix with almonds and
demerara sugar and scatter over fruit. Bake for 10 minutes.

Cook's Tips
———◊———

- The chicken liver stuffing goes equally well with jacket
  potatoes – and these can be cooked in the microwave for
  speed (see page 98).
- If red cabbage is unavailable use shredded white cabbage
  in the salad and add a sprinkling of caraway seeds for
  extra flavour.
- To skin tomatoes, drop into boiling water for a few
  seconds then peel.

MENU 5

——◇——

Speedy Spears
Cracked Wheat Salad

Fresh Pears with Parmesan

*The perfect menu when you know you're going to have
even less time than usual on the day itself – everything can
be prepared in advance leaving just the assembling and
cooking of the kebabs on the actual night.*

Total time: 30 minutes
In advance: marinate the pork for as long as possible –
preferably overnight – but even half an hour will be
better than nothing.

Speedy Spears

——◇——

If you start these pork and pepper kebabs the night before, and leave
the meat to marinate, it will be divinely flavoured when you grill it
the next evening. Some supermarkets sell mixed packs of peppers –
red, green, yellow and even black – which makes these kebabs very
colourful – but any colour will do.

Marinade
2 tbsp olive oil
1 wine glass dry sherry
1 tbsp white wine vinegar
1 tbsp soy sauce
1 tsp grated fresh ginger root
1 small onion, peeled and cut into rings
pinch salt

Kebabs
1½lb/700g lean pork, cut into chunks
4 peppers, seeded and cut into 1 inch/2.5 cm squares
4oz/100g button mushrooms, wiped
1 tbsp chopped fresh herbs
salt and freshly ground black pepper

Mix all marinade ingredients together. Place pork in a large bowl, pour over marinade and mix well to coat. Cover and leave overnight in fridge, turning occasionally, if possible.

Next day drain meat and reserve the marinade. Thread pork and vegetables alternatively on to 4 kebab skewers. Sprinkle over herbs and season with salt and pepper.

Place under a hot grill for about 10 minutes, turning frequently until browned all over and cooked through, basting with reserved marinade during cooking.

Serve on a bed of Cracked Wheat Salad.

Cracked Wheat Salad
——◇——

A salad with a difference. It tastes even better if you make it the day before.

8oz/225g cracked wheat
2 tomatoes, cut into little chunks
1 onion, peeled and finely chopped
1 clove garlic, peeled and finely chopped
1 tbsp finely chopped fresh coriander
4 tbsp oil
salt and freshly ground black pepper

Place cracked wheat in a bowl and pour over enough cold water to cover by ½ inch/1 cm. Leave to stand for 15 minutes, or until water has been absorbed, stirring occasionally.

Add tomato, onion and garlic. Sprinkle over coriander and drizzle over oil. Season with salt and pepper. Serve with the Speedy Spears.

Fresh Pears with Parmesan
———◇———

Quite the most spectacular combination of fruit and cheese. Buy Parmesan fresh in a wedge.

4 Comice pears
4–6oz/100–175g fresh Parmesan cheese

Let everyone help themselves!

Cook's Tips
———◇———

- Always keep a chunk of ginger root available – it adds subtle spiciness to many dishes.
- Use chicken instead of pork on the kebabs for a lower calorie main course.
- Use the same marinade given here to flavour pork chops and chicken joints for summer barbecues.
- If there's any Parmesan cheese left, wrap well, store in the fridge and use grated to flavour pasta dishes. Freshly grated Parmesan has far more flavour than the ready grated Parmesan bought in drums or packets.

MENU 6

◇

Rump Steak and Mushrooms
Boiled New Potatoes
Carrots Vichy

American Apple Pie

A luxury dinner for when you're feeling extravagant.

Make the American Apple Pie first. While it is cooking prepare the Carrots Vichy, and cook the steaks.

Total time: 45 minutes

Rump Steak and Mushrooms

◇

Not cheap – but every now and then everyone fancies a steak.

*2 tbsp oil
1 medium onion, peeled and finely chopped
2 cloves garlic, peeled and crushed
8oz/225g tiny button mushrooms, wiped
4 rump steaks
salt and freshly ground black pepper
wine glass red wine
watercress for decoration*

Heat oil in a pan and cook onion, garlic and mushrooms until soft. Remove with a slotted spoon and keep warm.

Turn up heat and flash fry steaks to personal preference. Season with salt and freshly ground black pepper. Transfer to a heated serving platter and top with the onion mixture.

Add red wine to the pan, stirring madly to scrape up any residue. Bring to the boil, then pour over the steaks. Decorate with watercress, and serve with boiled new potatoes and Carrots Vichy.

39

Carrots Vichy

————◇————

What's wrong with plain buttered carrots? Nothing – until you've tried these. No extra effort is involved either.

1lb/450g carrots, peeled and sliced
¼ pint/150ml chicken stock
1oz/25g butter
1 tbsp soft brown sugar
salt to taste

Place carrots in a pan with the stock, butter, sugar and a pinch of salt. Bring to the boil, then reduce heat and cook gently until all the liquid disappears and the carrots are lightly glazed – about 15 minutes.

American Apple Pie

————◇————

Use crisp eating apples as the slices will keep their shape and the filling won't disintegrate into a mush.

1½lb/700g eating apples, such as Cox's
juice of ½ lemon
2 tbsp flour
2 level tsp ground cinnamon
4oz/100g caster sugar
2oz/50g butter
6oz/175g frozen shortcrust pastry, thawed
1 egg, beaten
cream or ice cream to serve (optional)

Preheat the oven to 350°F/180°C/Gas 4.

Peel, core and slice the apples and sprinkle with lemon juice. Mix the flour, cinnamon and 3oz/75g sugar together in a plastic bag. Add apple slices and shake to coat them in the mixture.

Arrange apple slices in a 2 pint/1.1 litre pie dish and dot with butter. Roll out the pastry to fit the top of the dish. Trim to fit pie dish generously, then crinkle up the edges with thumb and forefinger. Cut out pastry shapes with scraps to decorate the top, if liked. Dampen with water and secure.

Brush the pastry with egg and sprinkle over remaining sugar. Make three slits in the top of the pie to let the steam out. Bake for 35 minutes or until top is brown and glittering with a sugary crust. Serve with a dollop of cream or ice cream.

Cook's Tips

———◇———

- Choose equal-sized steaks for easy cooking — and to avoid arguments!
- Buy ready-cleaned carrots, if your conscience will let you.
- It's always worth decorating a pie — it gives it 'eat-me' appeal and only takes a minute using the pastry scraps.

MENU 7

—◇—

Cheater's Chicken
Green and White Tagliatelle
Broccoli

Bananas Baked in Rum

This menu does take a little time as the Cheater's Chicken takes an hour to cook, but it can be left to do so unattended.

Put the chicken in the oven when you arrive home from work or prepare the day before and reheat. Cook the broccoli and pasta when the chicken is almost ready.

Total time: 1 hour 10 minutes

Cheater's Chicken

—◇—

Nothing wrong with cheating, so long as you train yourself not to blush! The sauce is based on canned soup, but nobody will know.

2 tbsp oil
1oz/25g butter
8 chicken thighs
10oz/270g can condensed mushroom soup
4 tbsp single cream (optional)
8oz/225g button mushrooms, wiped and sliced
4 tbsp dry sherry
salt and freshly ground black pepper

Heat oil and butter in a large flameproof casserole. Brown chicken pieces on all sides.

Mix soup with remaining ingredients, pour over chicken and season. Cover and bake at 375°F/190°C/Gas 5 for 1 hour – or until chicken is cooked through. Serve with broccoli and tagliatelle.

Green and White Tagliatelle
———◇———

Choose a mixture of green and white tagliatelle and cook as directed on the packet. You will need about 12oz/350g. Drain and stir through a good knob of butter and some chopped fresh chives.

Broccoli
———◇———

Trim and cook the broccoli as usual. If you have a steamer you could steam it over the pasta.

Bananas Baked in Rum
———◇———

A satisfying hot pud made with the minimum of effort.

4 bananas
juice of half lemon
4 tbsp dark rum
2 tbsp demerara sugar
a light sprinkling of ground cinnamon
2oz/50g butter

Preheat the oven to 400°F/200°C/Gas 6.

Peel and halve bananas lengthways and place in a shallow oven-proof dish. Mix together lemon juice and rum and pour over bananas. Sprinkle over the sugar and cinamon and dot with butter. Cover with foil and bake for 10 minutes.

Cook's Tips
———◇———

- Experiment with different flavoured soups for a variation on Cheater's Chicken.
- You could use chicken drumsticks instead of thighs . . .
- . . . And vermouth instead of sherry.

MENU 8

◇

Popeye's Pie
Tossed Chunky Green Salad

Ice Cream with Raspberry Sauce

A light and easy-to-prepare menu mostly made from storecupboard ingredients.

Make the salad while the tart is cooking.

Total time: 1 hour
In advance: the Raspberry Sauce can be made in
advance, if preferred.

Popeye's Pie

◇

A flavourful spinach and bacon tart which you will want to make again and again. It can also serve as a first course when made as individual tarts; small pieces make good bites to serve with drinks.

1lb/450g frozen leaf spinach, thawed
6oz/175g frozen shortcrust pastry, thawed
8oz/225g streaky bacon, de-rinded and roughly chopped
½ pint/300ml single cream
2 eggs
salt and freshly ground black pepper
freshly grated nutmeg
2oz/50g Cheddar cheese, grated

Press spinach in a sieve with the back of a spoon to extract as much water as possible.

Lightly oil a 9 inch/23 cm flan tin. Roll out pastry on a lightly floured board and line tin. Cover and chill for a minimum of 15 minutes. Prick base all over with a fork and line with greaseproof paper. Fill with baking beans and bake blind at 400°F/200°C/Gas 6 for 7 minutes.

Meanwhile, fry bacon in its own fat until crispy. While it is frying, place cream in a bowl and beat in the eggs. Season well with salt, pepper and about four good gratings of nutmeg. Stir in most of the cheese, reserving about a tablespoon.

Spread spinach over the base of the pastry case. Sprinkle over bacon then pour in egg and cream mix. Scatter reserved cheese over the top. Reduce oven temperature to 375°F/190°C/Gas 5 and bake for 35 minutes or until set. Serve hot, warm or cold.

Tossed Chunky Green Salad
———◇———

Crisp green salad vegetables in a Mustard Vinaigrette. Spring onion tassles are made in no time and make the salad look extra special.

½ Iceberg or Webb's lettuce
1 green pepper
½ cucumber
2 celery sticks
1 bunch spring onions trimmed and made into tassles, if liked (see Cook's Tips)
1 quantity Mustard Vinaigrette (see page 18)

Discard any damaged outer leaves from the lettuce. Clean if necessary but it shouldn't need washing. Cut in small wedges and place in a serving bowl.

Cut the pepper, cucumber and celery into chunks and add to the bowl, with the spring onion tassles.

Pour Mustard Vinaigrette over salad just before serving and toss.

Ice Cream and Raspberry Sauce

———◇———

An easy-to-make fruity sauce to serve with ice cream.

8oz/225g fresh raspberries
1oz/25g caster sugar
1 tbsp vermouth (optional)
ice cream

Purée raspberries in a food processor with sugar and vermouth. Strain through a nylon sieve to remove pips. Pour over ice cream scoops.

Cook's Tips

———◇———

- Frozen spinach can be thawed in a microwave. Follow packet instructions.
- See page 15 for how to reduce the chilling time of the pastry. Alternatively use a bought flan case for speed.
- Make spring onion tassles by slicing about a third of the way down the green part of each onion several times. Leave in a bowl of cold water for 10 minutes and the tassles will curl.
- Frozen or tinned raspberries can be used to make the sauce.
- You can always cheat and use a bought fruit sauce to serve with ice cream. Keep a jar in stock for emergencies.

MENU 9

---◇---

Fish in a Casket
Mushrooms with Lemon and Parsley

Oranges in Caramel

Here's a tasty fish meal with a fruity ending.

First prepare the Mushrooms with Lemon and Parsley and then the Oranges in Caramel. Leave both to chill in the fridge while you make the Fish in a Casket.

Total time: 45 minutes
In advance: make the Oranges in Caramel the night or morning before, if possible.

Fish in a Casket

---◇---

For a more economical meal, use just 1oz/25g prawns and add more white fish. Even a few prawns will give a feeling of luxury.

8 medium-size vol au vent cases or 4 large ones
¾ pint/450ml milk
8oz/225g white fish fillet
1oz/25g butter
1 small onion, peeled and finely chopped
1oz/25g flour
2 tbsp soured cream (optional)
½ level tsp dried dill
pinch cayenne pepper
salt and freshly ground black pepper
4oz/100g peeled prawns (optional)
parsley sprigs to decorate

Preheat oven to 400°F/200°C/Gas 6.

Place frozen vol au vent cases on a baking sheet and brush tops with milk. Bake for 15 minutes or until risen and golden. Remove from oven and leave to cool on a wire rack. Prise out the lids with the point of a knife.

While the vol au vents are cooking, poach the fish in milk for about 10 minutes, or until cooked through. Drain and reserve the liquor. Skin the fish and remove any bones, then flake.

Melt the butter and gently fry onion until soft. Stir in flour and cook for one minute. Remove from heat and stir in reserved poaching liquor, return to heat and stir until thickened.

Stir in the soured cream to make the sauce extra delicious, but to save money and calories, leave it out. Add flaked fish, dill, cayenne, salt and pepper to taste. If you're using 4oz/100g prawns add three-quarters of them now. Stir gently.

Spoon mixture into vol au vent cases and place a couple of prawns on each. Replace lids. Pop back in the oven to heat through. Decorate with parsley sprigs.

Mushrooms with Lemon and Parsley
———◇———

A fresh tasting, meaty kind of salad which goes with practically anything.

8oz/225g button mushrooms, wiped
½ small Spanish onion, peeled and finely chopped
1 tbsp finely chopped fresh parsley
4 tbsp sunflower oil
1 tbsp lemon juice
1 tbsp soy sauce
1 tbsp sherry
salt and freshly ground black pepper

Cut stalks off mushrooms and place the caps in a serving dish. Sprinkle over the onion and parsley.

Mix together oil, lemon juice, soy sauce, sherry, salt and pepper and pour over mushrooms. Toss well and leave to chill in the fridge for 30 minutes before serving.

Oranges in Caramel
———◇———

Simple and fruity, this is always a successful pud and goes down particularly well after pastry in the main course.

4 large oranges
4 tbsp sugar
¼ pint/150 ml water

Carefully peel the oranges with a serrated edged knife removing all traces of pith.

Cut oranges into thin circular slices, saving as much juice as possible and discarding any pips. Arrange slices in overlapping circles on a flat plate. Pour over the juice.

Put sugar and water in a pan. Stir over a low heat until sugar dissolves. Bring to the boil and boil fast until the syrup turns golden brown.

Drizzle syrup over orange slices and watch it solidify. Chill overnight if possible to allow the caramel to dissolve into the orange juice and make a delicious sauce. Serve on its own or with fresh cream.

Cook's Tips
———◇———

- Frozen fish is just as good as fresh for the Fish in a Casket.
- Use ready-cooked packet vol au vent cases for even more speed.
- Don't throw away mushroom stalks from the salad. Instead, why not chop them and use in the vol au vent filling, frying them with the onions? Or save them to add to a stock or soup.
- Instead of Caramel serve the oranges in Grand Marnier. Simply pour 4 tablespoons of Grand Marnier over the sliced oranges, cover and chill in the fridge until needed.

MENU 10

———◇———

Tomato, Avocado and Mozzarella Salad

Mackerel with Gooseberry and Apple Sauce
Hot Herby French Bread

*A cheap and cheerful midweek menu of a starter and main
course. Each can be made in minutes.*

Make the Gooseberry and Apple Sauce first. Then prepare
the herb bread and wrap in foil, so it's ready to bake in the
oven while the fish is grilling. Make the salad next.

Total time: 30 minutes

Tomato Avocado and Mozzarella Salad

———◇———

This is an orderly salad, arranged in neat lines of overlapping slices of
red, green and white.

1 beefsteak tomato
7oz/200g Mozzarella cheese
1 large ripe avocado
4 tbsp Herb Vinaigrette made with shredded basil (see page 18)

Slice tomato, mozzarella and avocado into even-sized pieces and
arrange on an oval platter. Drizzle over dressing.

Mackerel
with Gooseberry and Apple Sauce

———◇———

The sauce is fruity and slightly sharp – a good contrast to the oiliness of the mackerel. It can be made in advance and reheated.

Gooseberry and Apple Sauce
8oz/225g frozen gooseberries
1 large cooking apple, peeled, cored and sliced
1 tbsp sugar
1oz/25g butter
lemon juice (optional)
salt and freshly ground black pepper

4 medium-sized mackerel, gutted and cleaned but heads left on
salt and freshly ground black pepper

For the sauce, place gooseberries in a saucepan with enough water to cover. Poach for about 5 minutes or until soft. Drain, discarding the liquid, and transfer gooseberries to a serving bowl.

Put apple slices in the saucepan and cook slowly with no extra water until they turn mushy. Add sugar and mash any bits of apple in. Add the gooseberries, butter and, if necessary, a dash of lemon juice to taste (it may be sharp enough already) and mix together. Season with salt and pepper and spoon back into the bowl.

Slash the mackerel deeply three times on each side, season with salt and pepper and grill for about 12 minutes turning over halfway through the cooking time. Serve with the Gooseberry and Apple Sauce and Hot Herby French Bread.

Hot Herby French Bread

———◇———

A delectable aroma from the cooker will set taste buds quivering when you make this.

1 small French loaf

Herb butter
4oz/100g butter, softened
1 tbsp each finely chopped fresh parsley, thyme and chives
salt and freshly ground black pepper

Preheat oven to 400°F/200°C/Gas 6.

Mix together the butter, herbs and seasoning.

Cut loaf into slices. Spread one side of each slice with butter, then re-assemble the loaf. Wrap tightly in foil and bake for about 10 minutes or until heated through and the butter has melted into the bread.

Cooks' Tips for Menu 10 appear on page 54.

Cook's Tips

————◇————

- For a smoother Gooseberry and Apple Sauce, purée in a food processor or push through a sieve.
- To soften butter, microwave on HIGH for 5 seconds, but keep your eye on it.
- For an even speedier version of the herb bread, cut the loaf horizontally, spread with Herb Butter and bake in foil, then slice *afterwards*.
- Vary the herbs used in the Herb Butter. Use a mixture or just one herb – chives or parsley on their own are particularly good. And you don't have to use just herbs – beat any of the following ingredients into the softened butter and spread on French bread to make a tasty accompaniment to salads and stews. Or wrap in foil and shape into small cylinders while still soft, then chill. When hard, unwrap and slice into pats to serve on top of steaks, chops, jacket potatoes, and vegetables.

Garlic Butter
4oz/100g salted butter, softened
2 cloves garlic, peeled and crushed
1 small bunch parsley, finely chopped

Anchovy Butter
4oz/100g unsalted butter, softened
2 tsp anchovy essence
3 anchovy fillets, cut into tiny slivers

Olive and Red Pimiento Butter
4oz/100g unsalted butter, softened
2oz/50g green olives stuffed with red pimientos, very finely chopped or put through a garlic press

Onion Butter
4oz/100g salted butter, softened
1 small onion, peeled and finely grated
1 tsp lemon juice
lots of freshly ground black pepper

MENU 11

---◇---

Hot Leeks Vinaigrette

Chicken with Lime and Tarragon
Pasta Shells with Peas

A delightful menu that's smart enough for a dinner party, particularly if you add a dessert or cheese course.

Make the Leeks Vinaigrette in advance or while the chicken is cooking.

Total time: 30 minutes

Hot Leeks Vinaigrette

---◇---

A great starter which can be served hot or cooled and chilled overnight. It saves a lot of time and waste if you buy ready-trimmed leeks, even if they seem more expensive – you won't have to throw the tough green tops away.

1lb/450g leeks, washed and trimmed (thin ones if possible)
1 clove garlic, peeled and crushed
1 tsp French mustard
1 tbsp white wine vinegar
3 tbsp oil
1 tbsp finely chopped fresh parsley
salt and freshly ground black pepper

Cook leeks whole in boiling salted water for about 8 minutes. Meanwhile, put garlic in a screw-top jar with the mustard, vinegar, oil, parsley, salt and pepper. Shake together.

Drain leeks and press out as much water as possible. Arrange on a serving plate and pour the dressing over while they're still hot.

Chicken with Lime and Tarragon

———◇———

This always tastes special although it's cheap to make.

2 tbsp oil
1 onion, peeled and chopped
4 chicken breast fillets, sliced thickly
¼ pint/150ml chicken stock
¼ pint/150ml dry white wine
1 lime
2 level tsp dried tarragon
salt and freshly ground black pepper
3 tbsp single cream

Heat half the oil in a pan and fry onion until soft but not brown. Remove with a slotted spoon and reserve.

Heat remaining oil in the pan and brown the chicken slices all over. Return onion to the pan and pour over stock and wine. Bring to the boil and simmer, uncovered, for 15–20 minutes or until the chicken is cooked through.

Cut a slice from the middle of the lime to keep for decoration, if liked. Squeeze out juice into the pan. Add tarragon and seasoning then simmer for a further 2 minutes.

Add cream to pan and heat through. Serve from the pan or transfer to a serving platter and decorate with a slice of lime.

Pasta Shells with Peas

———◇———

Choose the tiny pasta shells and cook as directed on the packet. You will need about 12oz/350g. Drain, and when still hot stir through a good knob of butter and a handful of defrosted frozen peas. Sprinkle on a little chopped fresh parsley.

Cook's Tips

———◇———

- Make sure the leeks are washed thoroughly. Cut down vertically a couple of inches into the tightly packed white part. Rinse well under running water.
- To save time, if you already have a jar of made-up vinaigrette in the fridge use that instead of making the special dressing given here, which uses slightly different proportions of oil and vinegar and no lemon juice.
- If you put the lime in the microwave for 10 seconds on HIGH it will give more juice. This applies to lemons too.
- If liked, add lime zest to the sauce as well as juice to give an even more 'limey' flavour.
- Don't worry if you don't have pasta shells – any shapes like bows or spirals, or even macaroni or chopped spaghetti, will do just as well.

MENU 12

———◇———

Crusty Glazed Lamb
New Potatoes
Lemon French Beans

Pears with Chocolate Sauce

Chops are the quick and easy cook's standby, taking only a few minutes to grill. Here they are made extra tasty with a crusty glaze of wholegrain mustard and brown sugar.

Prepare the Pears with Chocolate Sauce first. Cook the beans while the chops are grilling.

Total time: 40 minutes

Crusty Glazed Lamb

———◇———

Serve these with baby new potatoes and lemon french beans.

4 lamb chops or steaks, trimmed if necessary
oil for brushing
salt and freshly ground black pepper
4 tsp wholegrain mustard
3 tsp dark brown sugar
fresh rosemary sprigs for decoration

Brush one side of the chops with oil and season with salt and pepper. Grill on this side for 7 minutes.

Meanwhile, mix together the mustard and sugar. Turn chops over and paint with the mustard and sugar mix. Grill for a further 3 minutes or until cooked to taste. Serve decorated with rosemary sprigs.

Lemon French Beans

—◇—

This dish is always popular and very quick to prepare.

12oz/350g French beans, topped and tailed
1oz/25g unsalted butter
zest and juice of ½ lemon
salt and freshly ground black pepper

Cook beans in plenty of lightly salted boiling water for 5 minutes.
  Drain and toss in butter. Sprinkle over lemon zest and juice and
season well.

Pears with Chocolate Sauce

—◇—

This is an extremely useful chocolate sauce. Dark, rich and glossy, it
can be served hot or cold and can be made in advance.

4 dessert pears
water to cover
1 tbsp caster sugar

Sauce
3oz/75g plain chocolate
2oz/50g caster sugar
1 level tsp cocoa powder
½ pint/300ml cold water

To make the sauce, melt chocolate in a pan with sugar, cocoa and
half the water. Stir and heat gently until smooth.
  Stir in remaining water and bring to the boil. Reduce heat and
simmer for 15–20 minutes or until the mixture is dark brown and
shiny.
  Meanwhile, carefully peel the pears leaving stalks on. Place in a
saucepan and cover with water. Add the sugar. Bring to the boil, turn
down and poach for about 15 minutes. Drain.
  Pour sauce over the pears to serve.

Cook's Tips

——◇——

- Dijon or made English mustard can replace wholegrain mustard in the Crusty Glazed Lamb if that's all you've got.
- You could always cheat and use bottled or canned new potatoes with their skins on instead of cooking fresh ones.
- Frozen French beans save on preparation time. Alternatively serve the lamb with sliced courgettes instead of French beans. They take less time to cook and can also be tossed in butter and lemon juice if liked.
- To save time use canned pears instead of poaching fresh ones.
- Make double quantity of chocolate sauce and store in the fridge. Use to transform ice cream or bananas.
- You could serve the pears with Raspberry Sauce instead of chocolate sauce (see page 47).

MENU 13

—◇—

Mushroom and Almond Risotto
Leaf Spinach with Gorgonzola

Melonitta

An all-vegetable meal like this one can induce feelings of great virtue in the traditional meat eater.

Prepare the Melonitta first and leave to chill in the fridge while you cook the main course. Make the Leaf Spinach with Gorgonzola while the rice is simmering.

Total time: 35 minutes

Mushroom and Almond Risotto

—◇—

This is not a true risotto, but who's arguing? It is, however, quite irresistible and very satisfying – as well as less bother than a genuine risotto.

2oz/50g butter
1 medium onion, peeled and finely chopped
8oz/225g easy-cook long grain rice
¾ pint/450ml vegetable stock
1lb/450g mushrooms, wiped and chopped
2oz/50g flaked almonds, toasted (see page 29)
1 tbsp finely snipped fresh chives
salt and freshly ground black pepper
2oz/50g Cheddar cheese, finely grated (optional)

Melt half the butter in a pan and fry onion until soft. Add rice and stir to coat in butter. Pour over the stock and heat to simmering point.

Cover and cook for about 15 minutes or until all the liquid has been absorbed and the grains are tender. Add extra stock or water, if necessary, during cooking.

Meanwhile, fry mushrooms in remaining butter until soft.

Stir the mushrooms into the cooked rice with the almonds and chives. Season with salt and pepper. Sprinkle over grated Cheddar cheese for a delicious melted goo on the top.

Leaf Spinach with Gorgonzola
—◇—

The Gorgonzola brings out a richness of flavour in the spinach.

1lb/450g frozen leaf spinach
½ oz/15g butter
good pinch nutmeg
2oz/50g Gorgonzola cheese, crumbled
salt and freshly ground black pepper

Cook spinach according to instructions on the packet. Drain thoroughly then return to the pan with butter and nutmeg. Heat gently until the butter has melted.

Add Gorgonzola and stir through until melted. Season, remembering that the cheese is salty, and serve.

Melonitta

—◇—

A simple and refreshing dessert.

1 large ripe honeydew melon, halved and seeded
4 tbsp Grand Marnier
a few fresh mint leaves, shredded
icing sugar for dredging

Cut the melon into bite-sized chunks or scoop into balls with a melon baller. Arrange in 4 dishes and drizzle over Grand Marnier. Chill until needed.

Just before serving sprinkle each dish with shredded mint and sift a little icing sugar over the top.

Cook's Tips

—◇—

- Unless there are vegetarians among you, you could use chicken stock instead of vegetable. For a special occasion substitute some of the stock with white wine.
- For the fastest risotto in town use canned rice. As it's already cooked, you'll only need a little stock to flavour it.
- Why not experiment and use a mixture of the different mushrooms available? Or look for dried porcini or other dried wild mushrooms. Soak in water for a few minutes before using. They won't need frying and any soaking liquid can be used to cook the rice in in place of stock.
- Gorgonzola is easier to crumble straight from the fridge.
- Use a food processor to chop the mushrooms and onion, and to grate the cheeses. Don't waste time washing the bowl between functions.
- If really pushed for time, don't bother to cut the melon into chunks; simply sprinkle each half with the liqueur, mint and sugar and serve.

MENU 14

—◇—

Pyrenean Pork
Special Mash
Green Salad

Baked Grannies

A delicious meal guaranteed to lure hungry diners to the table with the tantalising aroma of orange and sage.

Put the potatoes on to cook first. Make the salad and bake the apples while you are cooking the pork.

Total time: 45 minutes

Pyrenean Pork

—◇—

Pork fillet is a useful, fast-cooking and very versatile meat. Cheap too, if you consider how little waste there is.

1oz/25g butter
1 tbsp oil
1 small onion, peeled and finely chopped
1lb/450g pork fillet, sliced
grated rind and juice of an orange
3 fresh sage leaves, chopped or ½ level tsp dried sage
salt and freshly ground black pepper
¼ pint/150ml soured cream or stabilised yogurt (see page 17)

Melt butter with the oil and gently fry onion until soft but not brown. Add pork fillet to pan and fry until brown on all sides.

Sprinkle over orange rind, sage and seasoning. Turn down heat and continue cooking for about 6 minutes, turning the pork once.

Add orange juice, then stir in soured cream or yogurt. Heat through and serve with Special Mash and a green salad.

Special Mash
———◇———

King Edward potatoes make the best mash. Peel and cook in the usual way then mash to remove all the lumps. Add an egg and one tablespoon of grated Cheddar cheese. Or add Cheddar cheese and finely chopped spring onions. Or use up the last quarter tub of soured cream you've got left in the fridge with some fresh chopped chives. The possibilities are endless!

Green Salad
———◇———

Supermarkets offer quite a selection of salad leaves. Wash and dry them thoroughly (see page 112) or buy packets of assorted ready-washed leaves.

Just before serving dress with your favourite vinaigrette (see page 18) and toss gently.

Baked Grannies
————◇————

The advantage of using eating apples for baking is that they require less sugar than cooking apples.

4 Granny Smith apples, cored
a few raisins
brown sugar to taste
4 cinnamon sticks
2 tablespoons water
cream or custard to serve

Preheat the oven to 375°F/190°C/Gas 5.

Score around the equator of each apple with a sharp knife. Pack the cavities left by the core with raisins and sugar, then poke in a cinnamon stick. Place in an ovenproof dish and pour the water around them. Bake for 30 minutes. Serve with cream or custard.

Cook's Tips
————◇————

- Use sage sparingly – it can easily overpower a dish.
- Use instant mash for extra speed. The flavourings will disguise it and nobody will ever know that you didn't peel and mash the potatoes with your own hands.
- Baked apples take only 5 minutes in the microwave on high – but remember to score them first.
- Fill the apple cavities with mincemeat instead of sugar and raisins, if you have any.

MENU 15

—◇—

Chicken Indienne
Pilau Rice
Spiced Cauliflower

Chilled Mango with Coconut

For an evening when you're feeling a little bit spicy!

Prepare the mango for dessert first to give it time to chill, then make the Chicken Indienne. While it is simmering begin making the Pilau Rice, and while the rice is cooking prepare the Spiced Cauliflower.

Total time: 45 minutes

Chicken Indienne

—◇—

A mild curry with a rich and spicy sauce.

2 onions, peeled and chopped
2 cloves garlic, crushed
2 tbsp oil
4 chicken fillets, cubed
1 pint/600ml chicken stock
2 level tsp curry paste
1 tbsp tomato purée
juice of ½ lemon
salt and freshly ground black pepper
1 tbsp ground almonds

Cook onions and garlic in oil until soft. Add chicken cubes and cook until browned on all sides.

Stir in stock with curry paste, tomato purée, lemon juice, salt and pepper. Cover pan, turn down heat and simmer for 20 minutes, or until chicken is tender.

Add almonds, cover pan and cook for a further 2 minutes. Serve with Pilau Rice and Spiced Cauliflower.

Pilau Rice
——◇——

A tasty, pleasantly spiced rice to accompany the chicken.

3oz/75g butter
1 onion, peeled and sliced
1 clove garlic, crushed
6 cardamom pods
10oz/275g easy-cook long grain rice
pinch of cinnamon
pinch of ground cloves
salt and freshly ground black pepper

Melt butter in a pan, add onion, garlic and cardamom pods and cook until onion is soft but not brown.

Add rice and stir to coat in the butter. Add cinnamon and cloves and pour over just enough water to cover. Season with salt and pepper. Cover and cook over a low heat for about 15 minutes or until water is absorbed and the rice is tender. Add extra water if necessary during cooking.

Serve immediately.

Spiced Cauliflower

————◇————

Cauliflower is deliciously different when cooked with spices.

1 small cauliflower, broken into florets
2oz/50g butter
1 onion, peeled and finely chopped
2 tsps curry paste
1 tbsp tomato purée
¼ pint/150ml plain yogurt
salt and freshly ground black pepper

Blanch cauliflower florets in boiling salted water for 2 minutes.
   Meanwhile, melt butter in a pan and fry onion until soft. Stir in curry paste and tomato purée and cook for 1 minute.
   Add drained cauliflower florets and yogurt and season with salt and pepper. Heat through and serve.

Chilled Mango with Coconut

———◇———

There are a lot of fresh tropical fruits around these days. Use them to make fast exotic puds like this one.

1 lemon, washed
2 fresh mangoes
1 tbsp desiccated coconut

Scrape twirls of peel from the skin of the lemon using a canelle knife, if you have one. Otherwise grate coarsely.

Peel the mangoes, then cut them in half and remove the giant stone (see Cook's Tips). Slice the flesh. Squeeze on a couple of teaspoons of lemon juice, then sprinkle on the lemon peel and coconut. Chill well before serving.

Cook's Tips

———◇———

- There are quite a lot of onions to chop for this menu – so make use of your food processor if you have one.
- Choose fresh mangoes with no signs of bruising or damp patches. They should smell fragrant and yield slightly when gently pressed.
- The mango has the biggest, thinnest, flattest stone imaginable. To remove it, place the mango flat side down on a worktop. Put one hand on top and, using a sharp knife, slice horizontally along the length of the fruit, as close to the stone as possible, but underneath it. Turn over and repeat.
- No fresh mangoes? You could use tinned – but these tend to be a bit mushy. They're great puréed for a fast sauce, to serve with ice cream.
- You could use any other fresh tropical fruit – pineapple, pawpaw, or even bananas.

MENU16

—◇—

Tuna Fish and Cheese Soufflé
Julienne of Carrots and Courgettes

Baked Peaches with Rum

This is a cook and eat meal – it definitely isn't one that can hang about for latecomers or be made in advance.

Make the soufflé first. While it is cooking skin and stuff the peaches and chop the carrots and courgettes. Cook and dress the vegetables about 5 minutes before the soufflé is ready. As soon as it comes out of the oven, turn the heat down and put in the stuffed peaches.

Total time: 45 minutes

Tuna Fish and Cheese Soufflé

—◇—

Don't let anyone persuade you that soufflés are difficult – they're not. Once you've got the hang of it you can use just about any filling you happen to have with the same basic mixture. All you need is co-operative diners who'll race to the table when it's ready.

1½oz/40g butter
1½oz/40g flour
¾ pint/450ml milk
4 eggs, separated
2oz/50g cheese, grated (see Cook's Tips)
7oz/200g can tuna, drained and flaked
salt and freshly ground black pepper
½ level tsp dried dill
pinch cayenne
good grating of nutmeg

Preheat the oven to 400°F/200°C/Gas 6. Butter a 1½ pint/900ml souf-flé dish.

Melt butter in a pan, add flour and cook for one minute. Remove from heat and gradually add milk, stirring all the time. Return to heat, bring to the boil then simmer until mixture thickens. Cool slightly, then beat in egg yolks. Stir in cheese, tuna, salt, pepper, dill, cayenne and nutmeg.

Whisk egg whites until stiff. Beat two tablespoons into the egg yolk mixture to make it a little more liquid. Fold in the remaining white carefully.

Order the diners to be seated in 30 minutes, and place the soufflé in the oven. Cook for about 30 minutes, until set.

Julienne of Carrots and Courgettes
———◇———

A pretty dish of orange and green matchstick strips, just barely cooked and served dressed with butter and parsley.

1lb/450g carrots, peeled
1lb/450g fresh courgettes, wiped
1oz/25g butter
freshly ground black pepper
1 tbsp fresh parsley, finely chopped

Cut carrots into matchsticks. Don't peel courgettes but just cut them vertically into thin strips.

Plunge carrots and courgettes into a saucepan of boiling salted water for one minute – they won't need longer because the strips are so thin.

Drain, dot with butter and sprinkle over a grinding of pepper and the chopped parsley.

Baked Peaches with Rum

————◇————

Make this with fresh peaches, or even nectarines. It's a good way of using up stale cake crumbs, but you can use fresh if that's all you have.

4 large ripe peaches, skinned (see Cook's Tips)
1 tbsp rum
2 tbsp stale cake crumbs
pinch of ground cinnamon
1 tbsp soft brown sugar
cream or yogurt to serve

Preheat oven to 375°F/190°C/Gas 5.

Cut peaches in half and remove the stone. Mix together rum, cake crumbs, cinnamon and sugar and pack into the cavities of the peach halves.

Place in an ovenproof dish and bake for 15 minutes. Serve with the juices in the pan and cream or yogurt.

Cook's Tips

————◇————

- You can use any hard cheese for the soufflé. Try Cheddar or Parmesan.
- Choose tuna in brine instead of oil if you're watching calories.
- If courgettes are not available, make the carrots more interesting by cooking them in orange juice with a pinch of dried thyme.
- To skin peaches, plunge into boiling water for 2 minutes, then rapidly skin with a sharp knife.
- If fresh peaches aren't available substitute tinned.

MENU 17

—◇—

Kidney, Bacon and Mushroom Kebabs
Pitta Pockets
Cabbage and Onion Salad

Brown Sugar Yogurt

The pitta bread can be stuffed with the salad and meat and eaten with the fingers or served as an accompaniment to the kebabs for a more formal meal.

Make and dress the salad first, then assemble and grill the kebabs.

Total time: 30 minutes
In advance: make the pudding the day before, if possible.

Kidney, Bacon and Mushroom Kebabs

—◇—

Satisfying and tasty kebabs made in a flash.

8 rashers streaky bacon, de-rinded and halved
4 lambs' kidneys, quartered and trimmed
12 button mushrooms, wiped and stalks removed
oil for brushing
4 cloves garlic, peeled and crushed
1 tbsp finely chopped fresh parsley
salt and freshly ground black pepper
4 pitta breads

Lay a piece of bacon on a board, hold down with the back of a knife and pull the bacon with your other hand to stretch it. Roll up into a little tube. Repeat with remaining pieces of bacon.

Assemble kebabs by threading kidney, bacon rolls and mushrooms on to metal skewers. Mix garlic with chopped parsley. Drizzle oil along the length of each kebab, then sprinkle with garlic and parsley mixture and season with salt and pepper.

Cook kebabs under a hot grill or on a barbecue for about 10 minutes, turning until cooked on all sides. Serve with warm pitta breads and Cabbage and Onion Salad.

Cabbage and Onion Salad

Fine shreds of cabbage and onion in a tangy lime dressing.

½ white cabbage, finely shredded
1 small Spanish onion, peeled and cut into thin rings
½ tsp caraway seeds
1 quantity Lime Vinaigrette (see page 18)

Pile shredded vegetables into a bowl and sprinkle with caraway seeds.

Pour over vinaigrette and toss through, preferably 15 minutes before serving.

Brown Sugar Yogurt

———◇———

This is a quite spectacular pud of brown sugar marbling winding through yogurt and cream. It's easy to make and tastes like a dream. For the prettiest effect it's best made the day before, when it has time to set as well, but half an hour will do.

½ pint/300ml double or whipping cream
¾ pint/450ml natural low fat yogurt
4 tbsp soft brown sugar

Lightly whip the cream to soft peaks, then stir in the yogurt. Pour into 4 wine glasses and level the surface. Top each with brown sugar and leave in the fridge – overnight if possible – for the miraculous transformation to take place.

Cook's Tips

———◇———

- Warm the pitta breads to make it easier to open up the envelope cavity. Pop them in the toaster for 45 seconds, or in a warm oven for a few minutes.
- Shred the cabbage and onion for the salad in a food processor, if you have one.
- Use Greek yogurt with the cream for a luxury version of the dessert – it's rich tasting and creamy. Alternatively, substitute Greek yogurt for the cream for a healthier dessert.

MENU 18

—◇—

Zicky Meatballs
Ribbon Noodles with Tomato and Olive Sauce
Palm Heart and Red Pepper Salad

Chocolate Biscuit Ice Cream

A fun dinner consisting of meatballs served with noodles and a fragrant sauce of tomatoes and olives.

The Chocolate Biscuit Ice Cream can be made in advance or just before you need it. Make the meatballs first and while they are chilling prepare and dress the salad and begin to make the Tomato and Olive Sauce.

Total time: 50 minutes

Zicky Meatballs
—◇—

Choose good quality mince for these – the redder it is the less fat it has in proportion to lean. Or buy steak and mince your own, if you have time, in a food processor or mincer.

1lb/450g best quality lean minced beef
4oz/100g fresh breadcrumbs
3 tbsp fresh parsley, finely chopped
½ tsp freshly grated nutmeg
good pinch mace
salt and freshly ground black pepper
1 egg, beaten
wholemeal flour, for dusting
oil for frying

Put mince in a large bowl with breadcrumbs, parsley, nutmeg, mace, salt and plenty of pepper. Add egg and mix well, preferably with your (clean) hands. Press the mixture together.

Dust worktop with wholemeal flour, then decide what size balls you want. This amount will make about 30 walnut-sized balls or 16 golf-ball sized ones. Nip off lumps of mixture and roll into balls in the flour. The wholemeal flour adds an extra touch of nuttiness. Place balls on a tray and chill for at least 5 minutes.

Heat oil in a shallow pan and gently fry meatballs in batches. Don't be tempted to crowd the pan and cook them all at once, or you will reduce the temperature and they won't brown. Cook until browned all over – small balls will take about 5 minutes and larger ones about 10 minutes. Serve with noodles and the Palm Heart Salad.

Ribbon Noodles with Tomato and Olive Sauce

———◇———

The chunky sauce is flavoured with chopped black olives.

1 tbsp oil
1 onion, peeled and finely chopped
1 clove garlic, peeled and crushed
14oz/400g can chopped tomatoes
1 wine glass red wine
1 tsp caster sugar
12oz/350g ribbon noodles
few leaves fresh basil, shredded
1 tbsp black olives, stoned and finely chopped
salt and freshly ground black pepper

Heat oil in a pan. Add onion and garlic and fry until soft.

Stir in tomatoes, red wine and sugar and bring to the boil. Simmer for 10 minutes.

Meanwhile, cook the pasta in plenty of boiling salted water until 'al dente'. Refer to packet instructions for cooking time.

Stir basil and olives into sauce then season, remembering that olives are salty.

Drain pasta and pour the sauce over. Serve with Palm Heart and Red Pepper salad.

Palm Heart and Red Pepper Salad
———◇———

A delicious and colourful salad.

14oz/400g can palm hearts, drained
1 red pepper, seeded and thinly sliced into strips
1 small Spanish onion, peeled and cut into rings
1 quantity Vinaigrette (see page 18)

Arrange palm hearts, pepper and onion in a serving bowl. Pour over Vinaigrette and toss. Leave for 30 minutes to allow salad to absorb the dressing.

Chocolate Biscuit Ice Cream
————◇————

This is incredibly easy to make. You simply stir biscuit crumbs into vanilla ice cream. It's made so fast that the ice cream doesn't actually melt and the whole process is completed practically before you've had a chance to close the freezer door.

4 plain chocolate digestive biscuits
8oz/225g vanilla ice cream

Place the biscuits in a polythene bag and roughly crush with a rolling pin, still leaving them a bit crunchy. Take the ice cream out of the freezer, and mash the crumbs in as quickly as possible. Return to freezer then serve later, in scoops.

Cook's Tips
————◇————

- You can use white or wholemeal breadcrumbs for the meatballs. Breadcrumbs are made in no time in a food processor. Make in bulk and store the surplus in the freezer.
- Multi-coloured ribbon noodles always look pretty.
- Omit the olives from the tomato sauce if anyone has an aversion to them.
- You can personalise vanilla ice cream in other ways, by stirring in chopped nuts, dried fruit, chocolate chips or brown breadcrumbs that have been sprinkled with demerara sugar then caramelised under the grill.

MENU 19

—◇—

Grilled Cod Cutlets with Dill
Hot Potato Salad
Courgette and Tomato Salad

Soured Cream Treacle Tart

A healthy fish main course with a choice of two salads, followed by a luscious Soured Cream Treacle Tart.

The fish takes no time to cook, so make the pud first and while it's cooking prepare the salads.

Total time: 40 minutes

Grilled Cod Cutlets with Dill

—◇—

Cod cutlets encrusted with peppercorns and flavoured with dill and lemon for a tasty midweek supper dish.

4 cod cutlets about 1 inch/2.5cm thick, wiped and trimmed
lemon juice
sea salt
2 tbsp black peppercorns
1oz/25g butter, melted
a pinch or two of dried dill

Sprinkle cutlets all over with lemon juice and season with sea salt.

Crush peppercorns roughly in a pestle and mortar (or see Cook's Tips) then press the bits of peppercorn into both sides of each cutlet. Brush one side of the cutlets with some of the butter and sprinkle over a little dill. Grill for about 5 minutes on this side.

Turn cutlets over and brush with more butter and sprinkle with a little more dill. Grill for another 5 minutes or until cooked through.

81

Hot Potato Salad

——————◇——————

This is an unusual but very good way to serve new potatoes.

1½lb/700g new potatoes, scrubbed
4 rashers streaky bacon, de-rinded and chopped
6 spring onions, trimmed and chopped
double quantity Vinaigrette (see page 18)

If they are large, cut the potatoes in half. Bring a pan of lightly salted water to the boil and plunge them in. Cook until *just* tender – they shouldn't be too soft.

Meanwhile, fry the bacon in its own fat until crisp, then drain.

Drain potatoes and place in a serving bowl. Scatter over bacon and spring onions and pour over Vinaigrette while potatoes are still hot.

Courgette and Tomato Salad

——————◇——————

A colourful salad that complements the fish well.

8oz/225g courgettes, cut into ¼ inch/0.5cm slices
8oz/225g tomatoes, quartered
1 medium Spanish onion, peeled and finely chopped
about half quantity Vinaigrette (see page 18)
a little chopped fresh parsley

Bring a pan of lightly salted water to the boil and cook the courgettes for 2 minutes. Drain and allow to cool. Place in a serving bowl with tomatoes and onion.

Drizzle Vinaigrette over the vegetables. Toss gently to coat then sprinkle over chopped parsley.

Soured Cream Treacle Tart

————◇————

Soured cream in this recipe makes all the difference. Surprisingly, it takes the richness off the syrup.

8oz/225g frozen shortcrust pastry, thawed
8 tbsp golden syrup
8 tbsp fresh white breadcrumbs
juice of ½ lemon
2 tbsp soured cream

Preheat oven to 375°F/190°C/Gas 5.

Roll out pastry on a lightly floured surface and use to line a well buttered 8 inch/20cm flan tin. Prick base all over with a fork and line with greaseproof paper. Fill with baking beans and bake blind for 7 minutes (see page 15).

Mix syrup with crumbs and lemon juice, then stir in soured cream. Pour into pastry case and spread smooth. Return to the oven and bake for a further 20 minutes.

Cook's Tips

————◇————

- If you don't have a pestle and mortar, an effective way to crush peppercorns is to place them in a plastic bag and roll with a rolling pin.
- When making the Soured Cream Treacle Tart, dip the tablespoon in boiling water before spooning out the syrup. It will then slide easily off the spoon.
- You could always use a bought pastry case for the tart, and don't forget that a food processor makes quick work of breadcrumbs.

MENU 20

—◇—

Somerset Turkey
New Potatoes with Chives
Leaf Spinach

Fig and Walnut Crumble

A fruity menu that's made in no time.

Prepare the crumble while the turkey and vegetables are cooking. Put it in the oven to cook while you eat the main course.

Total time: 40 minutes

Somerset Turkey

—◇—

Tender chunks of turkey in a subtle fruity sauce of apples and cider.

2 tbsp oil
4oz/100g baby onions, peeled
2 cloves garlic, peeled and crushed
4 rashers bacon, de-rinded and chopped
1½lb/700g turkey meat, diced
seasoned flour, for dipping
¾ pint/450ml chicken stock
¼ pint/150ml dry cider
1 red-skinned apple, cored and diced
sprig of fresh rosemary
salt and freshly ground black pepper

Heat oil in a pan and gently fry onions, garlic and bacon for 2 minutes. Remove with a slotted spoon and reserve.

Toss turkey in seasoned flour (see Cook's Tips) and dust off excess. Add to the pan and fry over medium heat until browned on all sides.

Return onions, garlic and bacon to pan and add stock, cider, apples and the rosemary sprig. Simmer gently, covered, for about 20 minutes or until sauce thickens and turkey is cooked through. Season with salt and freshly ground black pepper.

Serve with boiled New Potatoes with Chives and Leaf Spinach.

New Potatoes with Chives
———◇———

Scrub potatoes and leave in their jackets. Boil as usual, drain then dot with butter and sprinkle with snipped fresh chives.

Leaf Spinach
———◇———

Fresh spinach is time-consuming to prepare, so use frozen leaf spinach. It can be cooked from frozen. Place in a pan with a knob of butter and sprinkling of grated nutmeg and seasoning. Cover and cook gently.

Fig and Walnut Crumble

————◇————

A variation on the fruit crumble theme, with chopped walnuts in the topping.

14oz/400g can figs, drained
2oz/50g butter
4oz/100g wholemeal flour
2oz/50g light brown sugar
1oz/25g walnuts, roughly chopped
custard, cream or ice cream, to serve

Preheat oven to 350°F/180°C/Gas 4.

Arrange figs in a 1½ pint/900 ml ovenproof dish. Rub butter into flour with fingertips until it looks 'crumbly'. Stir in sugar and walnuts. Spoon mixture over figs and bake for about 15 minutes or until the top is crisp and golden.

Serve with custard, cream or ice cream.

Cook's Tips

————◇————

- To toss turkey in seasoned flour, place a few tablespoons of flour in a polythene bag with salt and freshly ground black pepper. Add turkey and shake together.
- You can use leftover cake crumbs for the crumble topping.
- You don't have to use figs in the crumble. Substitute any canned fruit or pie filling you like. Frozen fruit would need cooking and probably sweetening to taste first.

MENU 21
——◇——

Drunken Pork with Watercress
Special Fried Rice

Toffee Bananas

An easy-to-prepare Chinese-style meal.

Marinate the pork first and leave for at least half an hour. Prepare the Toffee Bananas when they are needed, not before.

Total time: 45 minutes

Drunken Pork with Watercress
——◇——

Finely sliced pork steak is marinated then stir-fried with watercress.

Marinade
1 wineglass dry sherry
2 tbsp soy sauce
2 cloves garlic, peeled and crushed
4 pork steaks, trimmed and cut into strips
3 tbsp oil
1 bunch watercress, washed and stems removed

Mix together sherry, soy sauce and garlic in a bowl. Add pork and mix well to coat. Cover and leave to marinate for at least 30 minutes.

Drain the pork, but reserve the marinade.

Heat oil in a large frying pan or wok. Add pork and brown quickly on all sides. Cook for a further 5 minutes, stirring.

Add watercress leaves and marinade. Cook just until watercress has wilted. Season and serve with Special Fried Rice.

Special Fried Rice

—◇—

This extra-quick version uses canned cooked rice. You can add any finely chopped vegetables you like.

2 tbsp oil
1 small onion, peeled and finely chopped
1 clove garlic, crushed
4oz/100g button mushrooms, wiped and sliced
two 8oz/225g cans cooked rice
2oz/50g peeled prawns, thawed and drained if frozen
2 tbsp frozen peas
2 eggs beaten
salt and freshly ground black pepper

Heat the oil in a large pan and cook onion and garlic until soft. Stir in mushrooms and cook for 2 more minutes.

Stir in rice, prawns and peas. Cook, stirring until piping hot. Pour eggs over and mix through – the eggs will cook on the hot rice grains. Season and serve.

Toffee Bananas

—◇—

A crackly toffee coating encasing a soft and sensuous banana filling.

6oz/175g caster sugar
¼ pint/150ml water
4 bananas, peeled
lemon juice
1 tsp sesame seeds, toasted (see Cook's Tips)

Place sugar and water in a small pan, and bring to the boil. Cook for about 4 minutes until medium brown in colour.

Meanwhile, halve the bananas and sprinkle with lemon juice. Place on a wire rack over a sheet of foil.

Carefully pour the hot caramel over the bananas. Sprinkle with sesame seeds and leave to cool and set for a couple of minutes. Serve.

Cook's Tips

—◇—

- Wash watercress in salted water to weedle out any small insects.
- You can use any fruit for the toffee pudding, for instance apples, pineapple chunks or orange segments.
- Don't be templed to taste the caramel or test it with your fingers until it's had a chance to cool. It gets *very* hot.
- To toast sesame seeds, spread out on a foil dish and place under the grill for 30 seconds. Keep an eye on them as they brown quickly.

MENU 22

◆

Grilled Trout with Almonds
Mangetout or green beans
Tomato and Basil Salad

Lemon Pancakes

It's good to eat fish at least once a week – try this fresh-tasting meal.

Make the pancakes first, and keep warm, covered, in the oven. Prepare the salad and the mangetout while the fish is cooking.

Total time: 40 minutes

Grilled Trout with Almonds
◆

Trout is available all year round to make this light and healthy dish.

4 trout, cleaned and gutted
4 tbsp dry white wine
salt and freshly ground black pepper
1oz/25g butter, melted

Topping
2oz/50g butter
1oz/25g almonds, blanched
juice of an orange

Slash trout 3 times on each side with a very sharp knife. Drizzle over a little white wine and season with salt and freshly ground black pepper. Brush with melted butter.

Grill trout for about 4–6 minutes each side, or until cooked.

Meanwhile make the topping. Melt butter in a pan and add almonds. Cook gently until almonds are golden. Add orange juice and mix well.

Transfer trout to a warmed serving plate and pour over topping.

Tomato and Basil Salad
———◇———

A refreshing and fragrant salad.

2 beef tomatoes, sliced
1 small Spanish onion, peeled and cut into rings
1 tbsp shredded fresh basil
2 tbsp olive oil
1 tbsp white wine vinegar
salt and freshly ground black pepper

Arrange tomato slices on a shallow serving dish. Scatter over onion rings and basil, then pour over oil and vinegar – the way you do when on holiday on the continent! Season with salt and pepper.

Lemon Pancakes
———◇———

Everyone has the ingredients for pancakes in their storecupboard and fridge.

Batter
4oz/100g plain flour
pinch of salt
1 egg, beaten
½ pint/300ml milk
oil for frying

2 lemons
caster sugar for sprinkling

Sift flour and salt together into a bowl then make a well in the centre. Pour the egg and a little milk into the well and beat, gradually drawing in the flour from the edges of the bowl. Beat until smooth. Beat in the rest of the milk little by little.

Heat a little oil in a small frying pan – use just enough to coat the base. Pour in a thin layer of batter and swirl around. Cook on the underside until bubbles appear on the surface, shaking it about to make sure the bottom doesn't stick. Flip over using a palette knife – or if you're feeling devil-may-care, toss – to cook the other side.

Turn out on to a warmed serving dish, roll the pancake up and keep warm while you cool the remaining batter.

Serve the pancakes sprinkled with lemon juice and sugar.

Cook's Tips

———◇———

- Ask your fishmonger to clean and gut the fish for you.
- Fresh basil is best torn and not chopped – it gives a better flavour.
- Try not to overcook mangetout or green beans – they are best served when still a little crunchy. They're healthier that way too.
- Instead of using white wine for the Grilled Trout with Almonds, sprinkle over a little lemon juice or orange juice.
- Pancakes freeze well. Stack with greaseproof paper between each pancake. They make a quick pudding served with ice cream, syrup or fruit sauce. They can also be rolled up with various savoury fillings and served with a cheese or tomato sauce.

MENU 23

◇

Cheese and Onion Pie
Broccoli with Bacon and Fried Crumbs

Winter Fruit Salad

The beauty of this menu is that it can be made from mainly storecupboard ingredients – plus a fresh vegetable.

Make the Winter Fruit Salad first to give the sherry time to soak into the fruit. Prepare the vegetable dish while the pie is cooking.

Total time: 55 minutes

Cheese and Onion Pie

◇

Made with wholemeal shortcrust pastry, or a ready-made wholemeal pastry case, this is quite a substantial tart.

6oz/175g frozen wholemeal shortcrust pastry, thawed
2oz/50g butter
2 Spanish onions, peeled and sliced
2 eggs
3 tbsp milk or cream
salt and freshly ground black pepper
6oz strong Cheddar cheese, grated
freshly grated nutmeg

Roll out pastry on a lightly floured board to line an 8 inch/20 cm flan or quiche tin. Chill for a minimum of 15 minutes (see page 15). Prick base all over with a fork and line with greaseproof paper. Fill with baking beans and bake 'blind' for 7 minutes at 400°F/200°C/Gas 6.

Meanwhile, melt butter in a frying pan and gently fry onions until soft but not brown. Remove with a slotted spoon and reserve.

Beat eggs together with milk or cream and season with salt and pepper. Stir in grated cheese and nutmeg.

Scatter onions over base of flan case and pour cheese mixture on top. Bake at 400°F/200°C/Gas 6 for 30 minutes or until filling has set.

Broccoli with Bacon and Fried Crumbs

The little bit of crunch provided by the bacon and crumbs makes this vegetable dish rather special.

1lb/450g broccoli, trimmed
4 rashers streaky bacon, de-rinded and chopped
2 tbsp fresh white breadcrumbs
salt and freshly ground black pepper

Cook broccoli in boiling salted water for about 8 minutes until just tender. Drain and place in a warmed serving dish.

Meanwhile fry bacon in its own fat until crispy. Stir in breadcrumbs and fry until brown.

Scatter bacon bits and crumbs over the broccoli just before serving. Season with salt and pepper.

Winter Fruit Salad
—◇—

A useful salad when there isn't a vast selection of cheap fresh fruit about – or when the fruit bowl is looking bare.

> *2oz/50g no-soak dried apricots, halved*
> *4 tbsp sherry or orange juice*
> *2 eating apples, cored*
> *2 bananas*
> *lemon juice, for sprinkling*
> *1oz/25g flaked almonds, toasted (see page 29)*

Place apricots in a bowl with sherry or orange juice and leave to soak for 5 minutes.

Slice apples and bananas and sprinkle over lemon juice to stop discoloration. Add to the bowl and mix all the fruit together.

Sprinkle flaked almonds over fruit just before serving.

Cook's Tips
—◇—

- Use mixed leftover grated corners of cheese for economy.
- If you can't find the no-soak variety of dried apricots, use ordinary ones, but you will have to soak them overnight. Alternatively, a microwave will speed up the softening process. Place 4oz/100g apricots with ½ pint/300ml orange juice and a strip of lemon rind in a microwave dish. Cover and cook for 8 minutes on HIGH. Leave to cool.

MENU 24

——◇——

Wednesday Pot
Buttered Mangetout with Pine Nuts
Baked Potatoes

Quick Orange Cheesecake

A hearty cold weather meal that won't break the bank.

Put the baked potatoes in the oven first, then make the Quick Orange Cheesecake. Leave this in the fridge to chill while you make the casserole. Cook the mangetout just before you need them.

Total time: 1–1¼ hours depending on the potatoes. Everything else can be ready in half an hour.

Wednesday Pot

——◇——

A quick and tasty casserole of liver and bacon.

*1½lb/700g lamb's liver, washed, dried and trimmed then
cut into slices
seasoned flour
2 tbsp oil
8 rashers back bacon, derinded
1 onion, peeled and finely sliced
1 clove garlic, peeled and crushed
14oz/400g can chopped tomatoes
¼ pint/150ml beef stock
pinch of dried oregano
salt and freshly ground black pepper*

Crusty Glazed Lamb with courgettes and new potatoes *(page 58)*

Top Beef Stir-fry *(page 109), bottom* Drunken Pork with Watercress *(page 87)*

Tagliatelle with Garlic and Walnuts *(page 149)*

Salmon en Papillote *(page 137)*

Jungle Trails *(page 148)*

Tagliatelle with Garlic Sausage and Mushrooms *(page 160)*

Tropical Fruit Salad *(page 164)*

Pears in Red Wine *(page 166)*

Toss liver in seasoned flour and shake off excess.

Heat oil in a flameproof casserole and fry bacon until browned. Add onion and garlic and cook until soft. Add liver and cook quickly, stirring, to brown on all sides.

Pour over tomatoes and stock and add a pinch of oregano. Season with salt and pepper. Cover and simmer gently for 15 minutes.

Buttered Mangetout with Pine Nuts

———◇———

Don't cook the mangetout for more than 2 minutes or they won't be crisp.

12oz/350g mangetout
2oz/50g butter
1oz/25g pine nuts
freshly ground black pepper

Cook the mangetout in boiling salted water for 2 minutes. Drain and place in a warmed serving dish with the butter. Sprinkle over the pine nuts and toss with pepper.

Quick Orange Cheesecake
———◇———

Light, fluffy and delicious, this takes only five minutes to make using a ready-made sponge flan case.

8oz/225g low fat cream cheese
2 tbsp icing sugar
zest and juice of 2 oranges
¼ pint/150ml double cream
1 medium sized ready-made sponge flan case
orange slices or segments, to decorate

Beat cream cheese with icing sugar. Add orange zest and juice and mix well.

In a separate bowl, whisk cream until stiff. Fold carefully into the cheese mixture, then pour into the flan case.

Smooth the surface and decorate the top with orange slices or segments. Chill in the fridge until needed.

Cook's Tips
———◇———

- To toss liver in seasoned flour, place in a polythene bag with a few tablespoons of flour, salt and freshly ground black pepper. Shake together.
- To speed this menu up serve boiled or mashed potatoes instead of baked. Alternatively prick potatoes with a fork and bake in a microwave oven. Four large potatoes will take about 30 minutes on HIGH. Transfer to a hot oven for 5–10 minutes after cooking, to crisp the skins.
- The most suitable potatoes for baking are Cara, Desirée, King Edward and Maris Piper.

MENU 25
—◇—

Chicken Baronet
Tagliatelle with Chives

French Apple Slice

A tasty and satisfying menu.

Make the French Apple Slice first, then carry on with the chicken and finish with the tagliatelle, which needs little cooking.

Total time: 1 hour

Chicken Baronet
—◇—

Fillet of chicken with a tasty sauce served with herby pasta.

4 chicken breast fillets
seasoned flour
4 tbsp oil
1oz/25g butter
1 onion, peeled and finely chopped
2 cloves garlic, peeled and crushed
1 small green pepper, seeded and finely chopped
14oz/400g can chopped tomatoes
¼ pint/150ml dry white wine
3 tbsp white wine vinegar
1 tbsp tomato purée
salt and freshly ground black pepper

Preheat oven to 400°F/200°C/Gas 6.
Dip chicken in seasoned flour, and dust off excess. Heat 2 tablespoons of the oil in a flameproof casserole dish and fry chicken

until brown on both sides. Remove with a slotted spoon and reserve.

Heat remaining oil and the butter in the casserole dish and cook the onion and garlic until soft. Return the chicken to the dish with the pepper, tomatoes, white wine, vinegar, tomato purée and seasoning. Bring to the boil, cover and cook in the oven for 25 minutes.

Tagliatelle with Chives

———◇———

Cook tagliatelle in plenty of boiling salted water until 'al dente'. See packet instructions for cooking time. You will need about 12oz/350g. Drain and toss in butter. Stir through chives and season. Alternatively stir through chopped anchovy-stuffed olives.

French Apple Slice

———◇———

This is quickly made by topping puff pastry with slices of eating apple and glazing with apricot jam. It can be made in advance and reheated to serve.

13oz/375g packet frozen puff pastry, thawed
4 Cox's Orange Pippins, cored and sliced
juice of a lemon
2 tbsp sugar
beaten egg, to glaze
2 tbsp apricot jam

Preheat oven to 400°F/200°C/Gas 6.

Roll out pastry on a lightly floured board to a neat rectangle about ¼ inch/0.5 cm thick. Prick all over with a fork.

Arrange apple slices overlapping each other to cover the pastry, leaving a border of ½ inch/1cm all round the edge. Press them in lightly. Squeeze lemon juice over apple slices and sprinkle them with sugar.

Brush pastry border with beaten egg. Bake for about 20 minutes, or until pastry is is golden.

Meanwhile gently heat the jam in a small pan then push through a sieve. Remove the cooked French Apple Slice from the oven and cool slightly. Brush the apple slices with sieved jam to glaze. Serve with cream or custard.

Cook's Tips
---◇---

- Fresh tomatoes, skinned, seeded and chopped taste much better than canned in the main course. To skin plunge into boiling water for 30 seconds – the skins will then slide off easily. Halve, then scoop seeds out with a teaspoon.
- Fresh tagliatelle cooks more quickly than dried and tastes better too.
- No fresh chives? The green of spring onions finely chopped will do nicely. Don't forget you can freeze chives.
- Ready-to-roll puff pastry can be used instead of frozen.

Menu 26

—◇—

Greek Salad

Coddy
Yellow Pepper Rice

This is a particularly quick menu, with a starter instead of a pudding.

Make the Coddy first then the rice dish. The first course of Greek Salad can be made at the last minute just before serving.

Total time: 30 minutes

Greek Salad

—◇—

An appetising, crunchy starter. Tasty feta cheese makes an interesting and different salad.

Dressing
3 tbsp olive oil
1 tbsp lemon juice
salt and freshly ground black pepper

Salad
½ cucumber, diced
3 tomatoes, quartered
½ head celery, cut into chunks
½ lettuce, shredded
6 black olives, stoned
3oz/75g feta cheese, cut into cubes
1 tbsp fresh chopped coriander
lemon wedges, to garnish

For the dressing, shake oil, lemon juice, salt and pepper in a screw-top jar.

Arrange cucumber, tomatoes, celery and lettuce in a bowl and pour over dressing. Dot olives and cubes of feta cheese on top. Sprinkle with chopped coriander and serve surrounded with lemon wedges.

Coddy
———◇———

Cod is cheap and cheerful – but none-the-less really tasty and good for you.

1oz/25g butter
1 onion, peeled and sliced
1½lb/700g skinned cod fillet, cut into small chunks
2 cloves garlic, crushed
14oz/400g can chopped tomatoes
¼ pint/150ml dry white wine
2 tbsp chopped fresh parsley
salt and freshly ground black pepper

Heat butter in a deep frying pan and fry onion until transparent.

Add fish, garlic, tomatoes and wine. Sprinkle in 1 tablespoon of parsley and season with salt and pepper. Bring to the boil then simmer gently for 10 minutes.

Transfer to a warm serving dish and sprinkle over remaining parsley. Serve with Yellow Pepper Rice.

Yellow Pepper Rice

————◇————

The rest of this menu is so quick to prepare that canned cooked rice is used here to avoid holding things up.

2 tbsp oil
1 onion, peeled and finely chopped
1 clove garlic, peeled and crushed
½ yellow pepper, seeded and finely chopped
12oz/350g can cooked long grain rice
salt and freshly ground black pepper

Heat oil in a pan and cook onion, garlic and pepper until soft. Add rice, season, and stir well to combine.

Cook's Tips

————◇————

- No fresh coriander for the Greek Salad? Fresh finely chopped parsley will do, or a light sprinkling of dried oregano can take its place.
- Ask your fishmonger to skin the cod for you.
- If you prefer to cook the rice from scratch, follow the instructions on page 28.

MENU 27

—◇—

Poshburgers
Chips
Carrot and Apple Slaw

Grape Jelly

These home-made burgers are sensational and really quick and easy to make. They have a super meaty taste – and at least you know what's in them.

Prepare the Grape Jelly the night before. On the day, make the salad first and leave to chill in the fridge while the burgers and chips are cooking.

Total time: 45 minutes
In advance: 5 minutes the night before

Poshburgers

—◇—

Tarragon-scented chicken burgers served with a white wine sauce. Serve the burgers with a tomato sauce if you prefer (see page 20).

4 chicken breast fillets, roughly minced or processed
1 tbsp chopped fresh tarragon or ½ tsp dried
1 medium onion, peeled and minced or processed
zest of 1 lemon and juice of half a lemon
salt and freshly ground black pepper
1 egg, beaten
1oz/25g butter
2 tbsp oil
2 wine glasses dry white wine
¼ pint/150ml chicken stock
¼ pint/150ml soured cream or stabilised yogurt (see page 17)

105

In a bowl mix together the chicken, onion, tarragon, lemon zest and juice, salt and pepper. Stir in beaten egg thoroughly, to bind mixture together.

On a floured surface, mould the mixture into 4 fat burgers.

Melt butter and oil in a frying pan over medium heat. Gently fry burgers for 5 minutes each side, or until cooked through. Transfer to a warmed serving dish.

Pour wine into the pan and stir around to scrape up any tasty bits stuck to the bottom. Add stock then boil for 1 minute or until slightly reduced.

Stir in soured cream or yogurt and season with salt and pepper. Heat through to bubbling point.

Serve burgers with a boat of sauce and accompanied by freshly cooked chips and Carrot and Apple Slaw.

Carrot and Apple Slaw
——◇——

Matchsticks of carrot and apple tossed in a yogurt mayonnaise.

2 red apples, cored
4 carrots, peeled and cut into matchsticks
lemon juice
4 tbsp mayonnaise
2 tbsp yogurt
salt and freshly ground black pepper

Cut apples into quarters and then into matchsticks. Put into a serving bowl and sprinkle with lemon juice. Add carrots to bowl.

Mix mayonnaise and yogurt together and stir into the carrot and apple. Season with salt and pepper, and chill until needed.

Grape Jelly

————◇————

This is a good way of using up the end of a bunch of grapes.

6oz/175g seedless grapes
1 packet lemon jelly
¼ pint/150ml apple juice

Dissolve jelly in ¼ pint/150ml less boiling water than it says on the packet. Make up the difference with apple juice.

Put the grapes in a mould or bowl and pour on the jelly. Allow to cool then transfer to the fridge and leave to set overnight.

Cook's Tips

————◇————

- Make all the Poshburgers exactly the same size so that they take the same amount of time to cook.
- Vary the flavour of the burgers – with garlic, extra onion, spices and herbs.
- Oven chips are actually more healthy than deep fried ones as they are cooked without extra fat.
- Use a food processor to grate the vegetables for the slaw, instead of cutting into matchsticks.
- Red and green-skinned apples make the slaw look colourful and appetising.
- For a special occasion use white wine instead of apple juice in the Grape Jelly. Or you could use a mixture of apple juice and wine.

Menu 28

---◇---

Chicken and Prawn Soup

Beef Stir-Fry
Egg Noodles with Spring Onion

Fresh Lychees

Here's a fast do-it-yourself Chinese meal.

**Make the soup first. Cook the noodles while you stir-fry
the beef.**

Total time: 25 minutes

Chicken and Prawn Soup

---◇---

Tender chicken strips and prawns make a traditional Chinese-style
soup.

2 x 14oz/400g cans chicken consommé
1 skinless chicken breast fillet, cut into thin strips
1 tbsp cornflour
2oz/50g peeled prawns, thawed and drained if frozen
1 clove garlic, peeled and finely chopped
dash of soy sauce
freshly ground black pepper
1 egg, beaten

Pour consommé into a large pan and bring to the boil. Meanwhile,
shake chicken in a bag containing the cornflour, and dust off excess.

Add chicken to consommé and simmer for about 8–10 minutes,
until tender.

Stir prawns, garlic and soy sauce into consommé and season with pepper. Just before serving, pour in egg in a thin stream, stirring continuously. The egg will set into ribbons.

Beef Stir-Fry
———◇———

Strips of rump steak – go on, treat yourself – and vegetables in a spicy sauce. Remember that even-sized pieces of meat and vegetables will cook in the same amount of time.

2–3 tbsp oil
2 red peppers, seeded and finely sliced
6oz/175g mangetout, topped and tailed
4oz/100g button mushrooms, wiped and sliced
1lb/450g rump steak, trimmed and cut into thin strips
4oz/100g frozen sweetcorn, thawed and drained
6oz/175g Chinese leaves, shredded
3 tbsp soy sauce
pinch of five-spice powder (optional)
salt and freshly ground black pepper

Heat 2 tablespoons of oil in a wok or large frying pan and stir-fry peppers, mangetout and mushrooms for 2 minutes. Remove with a slotted spoon and reserve.

Add a little more oil to the pan and increase heat. Fry the beef quickly in batches, until brown on the outside and pink in the middle, stirring continuously.

Return vegetables to the pan and add the Chinese leaves. Sprinkle over soy sauce and stir in the five-spice powder, if using. Season and serve with egg noodles.

Egg Noodles with Spring Onions

———◇———

12oz/350g egg noodles
8 spring onions, trimmed and finely chopped
2 tablespoons sesame oil

Cook noodles according to packet instructions. Drain and stir through the chopped spring onions and sesame oil.

Fresh Lychees

———◇———

A super idea for pudding, in keeping with the meal's oriental theme. Buy juicy fresh lychees and serve piled up in a dish. Fresh lychees arrive in a brittle skin; peel this off with your fingers before eating. They also have a large stone in the middle – so watch your teeth!

Cook's Tips

———◇———

- Prepare all vegetables and make sure you have the other ingredients to hand before you begin stir-frying, as everything cooks very quickly.
- Don't overcrowd the pan when cooking the beef or all the juices will run out and the beef won't brown.
- Five-spice powder is a finely ground powder made up of five spices: star anise, cinnamon, fennel, cloves and Sichuan peppercorns. It is available in some supermarkets and specialist shops.
- If you can't find fresh lychees in the shops used canned ones and serve chilled.

MENU 29

—◇—

Blue Cheese and Spring Onion Omelette
Mixed Lettuce Salad

Black Cherry Trifle

A menu so fast that your hands will be a blur while you knock it up.

Total time: 30 minutes

Blue Cheese
and Spring Onion Omelette

—◇—

The spring onions give a peppery flavour but you can vary the filling according to what's in the fridge. It's quicker to make one large omelette and slice it into 4 rather than make 4 single ones.

2 tbsp oil
1 bunch spring onions, trimmed and finely sliced
8 eggs
3 tbsp water
salt and freshly ground black pepper
2oz/50g Blue Brie, pared and thinly sliced

Heat oil in a large frying pan and sauté the onions gently until soft. Meanwhile, beat eggs in a bowl with the water and seasoning.

Turn up heat and pour in eggs, swirling the mixture as you do so. Cook over high heat, dragging the cooked sides to the middle. Remove from the heat while the omelette is still slightly unset on top.

Cover the omelette with slices of Blue Brie and leave for just a few seconds to soften. Fold the omelette in half and transfer to a warmed serving platter. Cut into 4 and serve with Mixed Lettuce Salad.

111

Mixed Lettuce Salad

———◇———

Use any type of fresh, crisp lettuce – there are endless varieties available. For weekend entertaining dress the salad with a nut oil vinaigrette such as walnut or hazelnut – it's magical.

2 or 3 different sorts of lettuce
1 quantity Vinaigrette (see page 18)

Make sure the lettuce leaves are clean and dry before dressing. Any water that collects in the crinkles will dilute the vinaigrette. If absolutely necessary, rinse in cold water then dry thoroughly with kitchen paper. Otherwise simply wipe the leaves clean with dampened kitchen paper.

Drizzle the Vinaigrette over just before serving and toss gently.

Black Cherry Trifle

———◇———

A quick glance at the ingredients will assure you how fast this trifle is to make. It has a luxurious creamy texture and doesn't taste 'instant'.

1 packet trifle sponges or sponge fingers
a little Kirsch or orange-juice
1 packet instant custard mix
½ pint/300ml double cream
14oz/400g can stoned black cherries, drained
grated chocolate, to decorate

Break up trifle sponges and line the base of a glass serving bowl or 4 individual glass dishes. Sprinkle over Kirsch or orange juice and leave to soak in.

Meanwhile make up instant custard with half the quantity of water it says on the packet. Leave to cool. Whip cream until stiff and fold into the cooled custard. Pour cherries over the sponges then spread the custard evenly over the top. Sprinkle with grated chocolate and chill until needed.

Cook's Tips

———◇———

- Never cut salad leaves. Wipe them clean and tear apart to avoid bruising and discoloration
- For an extra quick Mixed Lettuce Salad buy a pack of ready-washed mixed leaves.
- Substitute Greek Yogurt for the whipped cream in the Black Cherry Trifle if you prefer. You can also use up any leftover stale sponge cake in place of sponge fingers. Chocolate sponge cake works particularly well.
- Canned black cherries are a good storecupboard standby. They make a delicious sauce to pour over vanilla ice cream when heated with their juice. Or drain and use to fill a meringue or sponge flan case, which can then be topped with whipped cream.

Menu 30

—◇—

Chicken Rockie
Brown Rice with Pine Nuts and Raisins
Chicory Salad

Ginger Biscuit Mousse

A substantial meal for a chilly day.

Make the pudding first and leave to chill while you prepare the chicken and rice. Make the salad while both are cooking and toss through the dressing at the last minute.

Total time: 45 minutes

Chicken Rockie

—◇—

Chicken joints are basted and served in a spicy barbecue sauce.

4 chicken joints

For the sauce
3 tbsp maple syrup
juice of half a lemon
juice of an orange
1 tbsp tomato ketchup
2 cloves garlic, peeled and crushed
2 tsp Dijon mustard
salt and freshly ground black pepper
good dash of Worcestershire sauce
2 wine glasses dry white wine or chicken stock

Preheat oven to 400°F/200°C/Gas 6.
  Place chicken joints in a roasting pan skin side up. Mix maple syrup, with remaining ingredients except wine or chicken stock and

brush a little of the mixture over each chicken joint. Bake for 35 minutes, or until cooked through, basting with more sauce throughout the cooking time until all is used up.

Transfer chicken joints to a heated serving dish. Pour white wine or chicken stock into the roasting pan and bring to the boil stirring with a wooden spoon to loosen any sediment on the bottom. Strain the sauce over the chicken joints and serve with the brown rice and salad.

Brown Rice
with Pine Nuts and Raisins
———◇———

Brown rice is more filling than white and makes a good nutty accompaniment to the chicken.

8oz/225g easy-cook long grain brown rice
1 tbsp oil
1 onion, peeled and finely chopped
1 tbsp pine nuts
1 oz/25g raisins
1 tbsp finely chopped fresh parsley

Put rice in a large pan of lightly salted boiling water and simmer for 20 minutes. Drain, then return to the pan off the heat with a clean tea towel placed in the top to cover the rice (see page 28). The steam will finish cooking the rice while you fry the onion.

Heat the oil in a pan and fry onion until soft. Stir into rice with pine nuts, raisins and parsley.

Chicory Salad

——◇——

A crisp and crunchy salad with a touch of bitterness.

2 heads chicory, washed and separated
4 spring onions, trimmed and chopped
1 tbsp finely chopped fresh parsley
4 tbsp Orange Vinaigrette (see page 18)
freshly ground black pepper

Mix chicory, onions and parsley together in a salad bowl. Toss through the vinaigrette. Season with pepper.

Ginger Biscuit Mousse

———◇———

A rich and fattening but really quick-to-make pud. It's best made an hour before serving and left to chill in the fridge.

8 ginger biscuits
1 pint/600ml whipping cream
2 tbsp whisky, optional
1 tbsp caster sugar
sliced stem ginger, for decoration

Place biscuits in a polythene bag and crush with a rolling pin.

Place the cream, whisky and sugar in a bowl and whip until stiff. Reserve a little whipped cream for decoration and stir the biscuit crumbs into the rest.

Pile into wine glasses and chill for an hour. Top with a swirl of cream and slices of stem ginger just before serving.

Cook's Tips

———◇———

- No maple syrup for the Chicken Rockie? Use runny honey instead.
- Use canned brown rice to save more time.
- If you're leaving the whisky out of the Ginger Biscuit Mousse, you could also omit the sugar and whip the cream with 1 tablespoon of syrup from a jar of stem ginger.

Menu 31
———◇———

Fisherman's Pie
French Peas

Stuffed Peaches

A straightforward menu with a traditional family fish dish for the main course.

Make the dessert first and leave to chill in the fridge while you concentrate on the main course. Cook the French Peas while the Fisherman's Pie is in the oven.

Total time: 50 minutes

Fisherman's Pie
———◇———

Mixed white fish and hard-boiled eggs in a cheesy sauce, topped with mashed potato. Instant mash is, needless to say, very quick.

1lb/450g cod fillets
½lb/225g smoked haddock fillets
¾ pint/450ml milk
1 bay leaf
blade of mace
a few onion rings
2 hard-boiled eggs, shelled and quartered
1oz/25g butter
1oz/25g flour
4oz/100g Cheddar cheese, grated
4 tbsp double cream
salt and freshly ground black pepper
freshly grated nutmeg
1½lb/700g mashed potato

Put fish in a pan with milk, bay leaf, mace and onion. Poach gently for 10 minutes. Drain the fish and reserve the poaching liquid, but discard the flavourings.

Skin, bone and flake the fish and place in a deep pie dish with the pieces of egg. Preheat oven to 400°F/200°C/Gas 6.

Melt butter in a pan and stir in flour. Cook for 1 minute. Remove from heat and gradually add poaching liquid, stirring well. Return to the heat and bring to the boil, stirring continuously until slightly thickened. Stir in cheese, cream and salt and pepper plus a good grating of nutmeg.

Pour sauce over fish and eggs. Spoon mashed potato on top and level with a fork. Bake for 20 minutes, or until top is golden brown. Serve with French Peas.

French Peas

—◇—

A transformation for the humble frozen pea.

¼ pint/150ml chicken stock
12oz/350g frozen peas
¼ small iceburg lettuce, shredded
4 spring onions, trimmed and finely chopped
pinch of sugar
salt and freshly ground black pepper

Heat the chicken stock in a pan and add all the other ingredients. Bring to the boil and simmer, uncovered, until there is barely any liquid left in the bottom of the pan.

Stuffed Peaches
———◇———

A no-cook fresh fruit pud to round off the meal.

4 ripe, firm peaches
4oz/100g curd cheese
juice of half lemon
8 ratafia biscuits, crushed
1oz/25g shelled pistachio nuts, chopped
2 tbsp runny honey

Halve peaches and remove stones. Beat cream cheese with a little lemon juice until smooth. Stir in crushed Ratafia biscuits, nuts and honey.

Spoon mixture into peach hollows. Chill for about 30 minutes or until needed.

Cook's Tips
———◇———

- Cook the fish in a microwave for extra speed, without the milk, bay leaf, mace and onion. Use the milk to make the sauce.
- You can vary the fish according to what's available.
- Use canned peaches in the pudding if fresh ones aren't available. Or use nectarines, instead.
- For a speckly Fish Pie topping, beat finely chopped fresh parsley into the mashed potato.

LEFTOVERS FOR EXTRA SPEEDY SUPPERS AND SNACKS

---◇---

What is a leftover, you may well ask yourself, apart from something nobody wants to eat? And is there really anything appetising you can do with it anyway – bearing in mind that the second attempt will almost certainly be served to the same ungrateful recipients who left it yesterday?

Some things just aren't as good second time round, so you may well find yourself having to do something new with it. This has to be carried out fairly fast however. Put it in the fridge covered with clingfilm, with a definite intention to transform it and more than likely you will throw it away, unused, in a few days' time.

Somehow this leaves you with a clear conscience. The one thing it's almost impossible to do is throw it away the moment it becomes a leftover – it's just unthinkable. So what's worth keeping that, hand-on-your-heart, you *will* use up?

Cold meat and poultry
Use it fast or freeze it, as cold cooked meat quickly loses moisture and flavour. Use in salads, and meat sauces for pasta etc. Or make spicy meatballs. Put in a food processor with spices and a little yogurt or egg. Process then shape into balls and serve with a tomato sauce (see page 20).

Cooked fish
Good as a base for pâtés, mousses, fish cakes and pancake and vol au vent fillings. Use with leftover rice to make kedgeree.

Cooked vegetables
Always try to make a soup from leftover vegetables. Simply purée in a processor or blender then add liquid – such as leftover gravy or meat or vegetable stock. Otherwise use up in stews, salads, bubble and squeak, rice and pasta dishes. Leftover cooked potatoes can be used up in fish cakes, or pie toppings.

Rice
It's almost worth making twice as much rice as you need as it keeps covered in the fridge for several days and freezes like a dream. It can also be used to make a fast salad, special fried rice, or rice-based dishes like pilaff or risotto (see the recipes on pages 61, 68, 88 and 128).

Egg whites and yolks
You never make meringues the same day you make mayonnaise, but the yolks and whites will keep for 3–4 days in the fridge, in a bowl covered with clingfilm. The whites can be used in a soufflé, mousse or omelette. The yolks are good for enriching soups and sauces (don't boil, though, once you've added them or you'll scramble everything), and glazing pastry.

Pastry
There are always leftover pastry scraps after you've lined a tin or made a pie. Puff pastry trimmings are best used at the time. Re-roll and cut into small crescents or other shapes. Glaze with beaten egg mixed with water and bake alongside the pie or tart. Cool and store in an airtight tin and use to garnish soups and stews, fish dishes or grilled meat. Shortcrust pastry trimmings can be wrapped and kept in the fridge for a few days as they are. If the occasion arises and you're serving soup, roll out into small shapes and poach in a little chicken stock to use as a garnish – they make pretty little dumplings.

Agreed, this is not the sort of thing the busy person *plans* to do. But it really is no extra effort when you are already cooking and it will add a plus to presentation on future occasions.

Cheese

Old hard cheese is always usable, not as the hard, shiny, yellow, cracked hunk you gaze at dismally, but grated and kept in a jar. Sprinkle it on things, make sauces with it, or just use it for good old fashioned cheese on toast. It doesn't matter if you mix several hard sorts together, after all variety is the spice of life. Soft cheese, like a knob of bent Brie or a sliver of leftover Dolcelatte, can also be used — pot it. Do this with hard blue cheese too. See page 124.

Cream

Always keep the end of a tub of cream and use to add a touch of luxury to soups and sauces.

Baked Eggs with Sherry and Cream
———◇———

This is a bit on the rich side, but it's very, very good as a starter or light supper dish and is a delicious way of using up a few spoonfuls of leftover cream.

Serves 4

Total time: 17 minutes

2 tbsp sherry
4 eggs
salt and freshly ground white pepper
4 tbsp leftover single cream

Preheat the oven to 350°F/180°C/Gas 4.

Butter 4 individual ramekin dishes and divide the sherry between them. Carefully break an egg into each and season with salt and pepper. Spoon over the cream.

Put ramekins in a roasting tin half filled with hot water and cook for 15 minutes or until the eggs are just set.

Potted Cheese

———◇———

Good as a sandwich filling or spread on hot wholemeal toast for a snack or first course. If using soft cheese like Brie or Camembert, remove the rind before grating.

Serves 4-6

Total time: 5 minutes plus chilling time

8oz/225g grated cheese (hard or soft)
2 tbsp dry or sweet sherry
1 tsp French mustard
pinch ground mace
pinch cayenne pepper
2oz/50g softened butter

Mix together the cheese, sherry, mustard, mace and cayenne. Stir in softened butter and pack into a pot. Cover and chill.

Salade Niçoise

———◇———

The perfect way to use up leftover cooked French beans. It's a substantial salad – just serve with crusty French bread for a complete meal.

Serves 4

Total time: 5 minutes

1 clove garlic, peeled and crushed
6 tbsp Vinaigrette (see page 18)
8oz/225g leftover cooked French beans
1lb/450g tomatoes, quartered
14oz/400g can tuna, drained
3oz/75g black olives
1 tbsp chopped fresh parsley

Put garlic in a salad bowl with the Vinaigrette. Mix well with a fork.

Put the beans in next, then the tomatoes. Break tuna into large chunks and add. Scatter over olives and turn over carefully without breaking up tuna. Sprinkle parsley over to serve.

Fish Cakes
———◇———

The advantage of tasty Fish Cakes is that they use up cold mashed potatoes as well as leftover cooked fish.

Serves 4

Total time: 20 minutes

1lb/450g cold cooked potatoes
1 tbsp leftover cream or softened butter
8oz/225g cooked white fish, flaked
1 tbsp chopped fresh parsley
a few capers, finely chopped
½ tsp anchovy essence
1 tsp lemon juice
salt and freshly ground black pepper
flour for dusting
1 egg, beaten
wholemeal flour for dipping
3 tbsp oil
Tomato or Tartare Sauce to serve (see pages 19 and 20)

Mix potato with leftover cream or butter. Add fish, parsley, capers, anchovy essence and lemon juice. Mix well and season with salt and pepper.

Dust a work surface with flour and shape the mixture into 8 flat rounds. Dip each round into egg then into wholemeal flour.

Heat the oil in a pan and fry the fish cakes, turning, until brown on both sides. Drain on kitchen paper and serve.

Monday Stroganoff with Noodles

———◇———

Quite a tasty disguise for leftover cooked meat. Serve with leftover cooked rice, if you have any, rather than noodles.

Serves 4

Total time: 15 minutes

1oz/25g butter
1lb/450g cold cooked meat (anything), cut into thin slices and then into strips
1 onion, peeled and finely chopped
1 heaped tsp mild made mustard
½ tsp dried dill
¼ pint/150ml soured cream or stabilised yogurt (see page 17)
salt and freshly ground black pepper
8oz/225g noodles

Melt butter in a pan. Fry onion until soft. Add meat strips and stir. Add mustard, dill and soured cream. Heat through and season with salt and pepper.

Meanwhile, cook noodles in plenty of boiling salted water until 'al dente'. See instructions for cooking time. Serve noodles with stroganoff poured over.

Spaghetti with Beef and Mushroom
————◇————

This is a wonderful storecupboard standby – keep a packet of spaghetti and a can of mince in the larder for a quick and easy supper. If you have any leftover cooked meat, mince or process in a food processor and use with any leftover gravy or stock instead of the canned mince. Add whatever else you might have left over that's suitable, like a few mushrooms or some chopped pepper, to make the sauce more interesting.

Serves 4

Total time: about 20 minutes,
depending on the cooking time of the pasta

12oz/350g spaghetti
2 tbsp oil
1 onion, peeled and finely chopped
2 cloves garlic, peeled and crushed
14oz/400g can minced beef, or minced leftover cooked meat and
leftover gravy
1 tbsp tomato purée
dash of mushroom ketchup
4oz/100g button mushrooms, wiped and sliced
pinch of dried oregano

Cook pasta in plenty of boiling salted water until 'al dente'. Refer to packet instructions for exact cooking time. Drain and keep warm.

Heat oil in a pan and cook onion and garlic until soft. Add mince with leftover gravy (if you have any). Stir in tomato purée and a dash of mushroom ketchup.

Stir in mushrooms and oregano. Simmer for 5 minutes. Check for seasoning. Serve spooned over spaghetti.

Turkish Chicken Pilaff
———◇———

A rather racey little rice dish made with leftover cooked chicken.

Serves 2

Total time: 25 minutes

2oz/50g butter
1 onion, peeled and finely chopped
½ red pepper, seeded and cut into strips
10oz/275g leftover cooked rice
10oz/275g cooked chicken
2oz/50g flaked almonds
2oz/50g sultanas
salt and freshly ground black pepper

Melt butter in a large pan and fry onion until soft. Add pepper and cook for a further minute.

Stir in rice and chicken and cook until heated through. Scatter over almonds and sultanas and heat for a further 3 minutes. Season to taste.

Spaghetti alla Carbonara

———◇———

This is a naughty combination of garlic, sausage, eggs and cream. Definitely not for dieters, but a good way of using up slices of ham.

Serves 4

Total time: 30 minutes

12oz/350g spaghetti
2oz/50g butter
1 clove garlic, peeled and crushed
4 slices ham, cut into slivers
¼ pint/150ml single cream
4 eggs, beaten with salt and pepper
1 tbsp fresh chopped parsley
2oz/50g freshly grated Parmesan cheese

Cook spaghetti in plenty of lightly salted boiling water until 'al dente'. See packet instructions for exact cooking time. Drain and place in a bowl with half the butter. Stir in and keep warm.

Melt remaining butter in a pan and fry garlic until soft. Add ham slivers and fry for a further 3 minutes or until browned. Stir in cream, season and bring to the boil. Add eggs and mix in. Pour over hot spaghetti and sprinkle with parsley and Parmesan. Serve with a mixed salad.

Yakky Dar
---◇---

Fast pasta supper dish using leftover cooked leeks. You could use other leftover cooked vegetables such as peas, courgettes, beans, sweetcorn or broccoli.

Serves 4

Total time: 15 minutes

12oz/350g pasta twists
6 tbsp Vinaigrette (see page 18)
4 hardboiled eggs, shelled and quartered
leftover cooked leeks
8 rashers bacon, grilled and cut into strips
3oz/75g grated cheese

Cook pasta in boiling salted water until 'al dente'. See packet instructions for exact cooking time. Drain and toss in Vinaigrette. Turn into a warmed flameproof dish.

Stir eggs, leeks and bacon into dressed pasta. Top with grated cheese and flash under a hot grill until brown and irresistible.

MICROWAVE MAGIC

———◇———

There is no doubt about it – the microwave is here to stay. And if you're a busy cook you will never stop being thankful for yours.

Not only is the trusty slave on hand to thaw solid frozen chickens and frozen prepared meals, soften butter and melt chocolate and gelatine, but it also does a great job of cooking vegetables, fish and chicken in a flash.

But it's not just a gadget. The microwave can also cope with fast gourmet dishes – like these treats following.

Note The recipes in this section have been tested on a 650 watt microwave oven. If your model has a lower output (i.e. slightly less power), then allow extra cooking time. If your cooker has a higher output (for example 700 watts) you will have to reduce the cooking times slightly.

Snipper Soup
———◇———

Parsnip soup with onions, garlic and coriander makes an excellent starter for a winter evening meal. It can also be served as a main course soup with thick slices of crusty bread.

Serves 4 as a starter, 2 as a main course

Total time: 25 minutes

2lb/900g parsnips, peeled and finely diced
1 small onion, peeled and finely chopped
1 clove garlic, peeled and crushed
1 tsp peeled and finely chopped root ginger
1 tsp coriander seeds, crushed
2 tbsp oil
2 pints/1.1 litre vegetable stock
3 tbsp double cream
salt and freshly ground black pepper

Place parsnips, onion, garlic, ginger and coriander seeds in a microwave bowl. Pour over oil and mix well to coat. Cover and microwave on HIGH for 6 minutes.

Add stock and microwave on HIGH for 5 minutes. Stir then microwave for a further 5 minutes or until parsnips are tender.

Transfer to a food processor and blend until smooth. Stir in cream and season with salt and pepper.

Return to microwave bowl and microwave on HIGH for a further 2 minutes until piping hot.

Polli Ali

———◇———

This is a delightful, aromatic, fruit curry with a mildly spiced sauce.

Serves 4

Total time: 30 minutes

1 tbsp oil
1 red pepper, seeded and cut into strips
1 green pepper, seeded and cut into strips
1 onion, peeled and finely sliced
1 clove garlic, peeled and crushed
1 tsp grated ginger
1 tsp turmeric
1 tbsp curry powder
1½ lb/700g skinless chicken breast fillet, cubed
1 tbsp seasoned flour
4 tomatoes, peeled and chopped
½ pint/300ml hot chicken stock
14oz/400g can mango slices, drained
salt and freshly ground black pepper

Place oil, peppers, onion, garlic, ginger and spices in a microwave bowl and stir to mix. Cover and microwave on HIGH for 3 minutes. Stir and cook for a further 3 minutes.

Toss chicken in seasoned flour and add to bowl. Microwave on HIGH for 5 minutes, stir then cook for a further 5 minutes.

Add remaining ingredients and microwave for a further 5 minutes, or until the liquid comes to bubbling point. Taste and adjust for seasoning if necessary. Serve with boiled rice.

Pork Normande

—◇—

Wholegrain mustard really brings out the flavour of pork and cooking it in white wine and cream makes this quite a sophisticated dinner party dish.

Serves 4

Total time: 20 minutes

2 shallots, peeled and finely chopped
1lb/450g pork fillet, diced
pinch of powdered sage
salt and freshly ground black pepper
1 wine glass dry white wine
¼ pint/150ml chicken stock
3 tsp wholegrain mustard
2 tbsp double cream

Put shallots in a microwave dish and place pork on top. Sprinkle over sage and season with salt and freshly ground black pepper. Cover and microwave on HIGH for 4 minutes.

Pour over wine and stock. Microwave on HIGH for 4 minutes. Stir then cook for a further 4 minutes or until pork is tender. Remove pork and keep warm.

Add mustard to cooking juices and microwave on HIGH for 2 minutes. Stir in cream. Pour sauce over pork and serve with little new potatoes.

Lightning Liver Casserole

———◇———

Liver can't be beaten for an economical and tasty dish. This quick casserole is perfect for a midweek supper.

Serves 4

Total time: 15 minutes

1 tbsp oil
1 onion, peeled and cut into rings
1 clove garlic, peeled and crushed
1lb/450g lamb's liver, cut into thin strips
seasoned flour
pinch of dried sage
¼ pint/150ml hot chicken stock
¼ pint/150ml red wine
salt and freshly ground black pepper

Place oil, onion and garlic in a microwave bowl. Stir to mix. Microwave on HIGH for 2 minutes or until onion is soft.

Dip liver into seasoned flour and shake off excess. Add to bowl and microwave on HIGH for 3 minutes then stir in sage.

Mix hot stock with wine and pour over liver. Cook on HIGH for a further 4 minutes. Season with salt and pepper and serve with new potatoes or rice.

Seafarer's Supper
———◇———

Crunchy-topped haddock in a creamy sauce flavoured with cheese and nutmeg.

Serves 4

Total time: 25 minutes

1oz/25g butter
1oz/25g flour
½ pint/300ml milk
salt and white pepper
freshly grated nutmeg
3oz/75g Cheddar cheese, grated
3 tbsp double cream (optional)
4 haddock fillets, skinned
3 tbsp cornflakes, crushed
1 tbsp fresh white breadcrumbs, toasted
2 tbsp finely chopped almonds

Place butter, flour and milk in a microwave bowl. Microwave on HIGH for 6 minutes or until sauce boils and thickens, whisking every minute.

Season with salt, pepper and nutmeg and add 2oz/50g grated cheese. Microwave on HIGH for a further minute or until cheese has melted. Stir in cream, if using, and leave to cool slightly.

Place haddock fillets in a shallow microwave dish big enough to take all the fish in one layer. Pour over sauce and microwave on HIGH for 6 minutes. Mix remaining cheese with cornflakes, crumbs and nuts and sprinkle over fish. Microwave on HIGH for a further 2 minutes. Serve with a green salad.

Salmon en Papillote
———◇———

A very simple-to-prepare dish of delicious and healthy salmon fillets baked in greaseproof paper parcels.

Serves 4

Total time: 30 minutes

4 small Scottish salmon fillets
juice of 1 lemon
salt and freshly ground black pepper
1 carrot, cut into fine sticks
½ red pepper, seeded and cut into fine sticks
1 courgette, cut into fine sticks
1 leek, cut into fine sticks
1oz/25g butter
1 orange, cut into wedges

Cut 4 pieces of greaseproof paper 10 × 15 inches/25 × 38cm. Place a salmon fillet in the centre of each. Squeeze lemon juice over and season generously.

Scatter vegetable sticks over centre of each fillet then place a small knob of butter on top. Fold greaseproof paper around salmon into loose parcels, tucking the ends underneath.

Place parcels in a circle in a microwave dish and cook on HIGH for 6½ minutes until just cooked through (as shown in the photograph opposite page 65) or until cooked to your liking.

Place the parcels on 4 dinner plates and let each diner open their own. Serve with orange wedges to squeeze over the salmon and accompany with new potatoes and a selection of lightly cooked vegetables.

Tandoori Chicken
————◇————

Forget clay ovens, which are the traditional way of cooking this Indian dish. It's easily made in a microwave and tastes just as authentic, especially if you finish it off under a hot grill to give it the charred look.

Serves 4

Total time: 15 minutes
In advance: marinate the chicken at least 30 minutes before cooking the dish.

Marinade
¼ pint/150ml natural yogurt
juice of ½ lemon
2 tbsp tandoori paste
pinch of paprika
pinch of ground coriander

4 chicken joints, skinned
salt

Mix the marinade ingredients together. Make small slashes with a sharp knife in the chicken joints to help them absorb the flavour of the marinade, and rub with a little salt. Place in a deep bowl and pour over the marinade. Leave for at least 30 minutes, longer if possible.

Remove chicken from the marinade and place in a microwave dish. Microwave on HIGH for 12 minutes or until cooked through, basting with marinade throughout the cooking time.

Place under a pre-heated grill for 1 minute to get the charred effect. Serve with rice or a mixed salad.

Panic Pudding

——◇——

A light and airy whirlwind sponge pud with a hint of ginger and an apricot topping.

Serves 4

Total time: 12 minutes

4 tbsp apricot jam
2 tbsp Golden Syrup
4oz/100g unsalted butter
2 tsp crystallised stem ginger, finely chopped
2oz/50g caster sugar
2 eggs, beaten
4oz/100g self raising flour, sifted

Grease a 2 pint/1.1 litre microwave pudding basin and spread apricot jam around the base.

Place syrup, butter and ginger in another microwave bowl and microwave on HIGH for 30 seconds. Stir then microwave for a further 30 seconds or until melted.

Beat in all the sugar and half the egg, then beat in 1 tablespoon of flour. Next beat in remaining egg and fold in remaining flour. Pour on top of jam in pudding bowl and microwave on HIGH for 3 minutes or until a skewer inserted in the centre comes out clean.

Leave to stand for 5 minutes. Unmould on to a serving plate and serve with custard.

139

Carrot Cake

————◇————

Grated carrot not only makes an unusual tasty cake, but keeps it wonderfully moist. It's quick to mix too.

Serves 8

Total time: 20 minutes

Cake
3 eggs, beaten
2oz/50g wholemeal flour
4oz/100g self raising flour
6oz/175g butter, softened
6oz/175g demerara sugar
zest and juice of 1 lemon
1 level tsp ground cinnamon
4 large carrots, peeled and grated

Topping
6oz/175g cream cheese
1 tsp runny honey
1 tbsp lemon juice

Put all the cake ingredients except the grated carrot into a large bowl and beat together until well blended. Then fold in the grated carrot.

Spoon the mixture into a greased 7 inch/18cm round microwave cake dish and microwave on HIGH for 10 minutes. Stand 1 minute then turn out on to a wire rack to cool.

For the topping, beat together all the ingredients until smooth, then spread over the top of the cooled cake.

VEGETARIAN VISITORS

---◇---

The trend towards eating more vegetables, or even turning completely vegetarian is no longer considered the cranky obsession it used to be.

Diet has changed radically over the last decade. Meat – in particular red meat – is eaten less frequently and many people eat at least one completely vegetarian meal a week.

For the working cook this is a bonus. Vegetables are quicker and easier to cook than meat, and are cheaper too.

It's useful to have a store of quick non-meat recipes to turn to when faced with vegetarian visitors. Here are recipes for starters, main course and side salads. Menus 8, 13, 23 and 29 are also vegetarian and a number of the other menus contain fish rather than meat in the main course.

Gazpacho
———◇———

A tasty no-cook vegetable soup from Andalusia which is served chilled.

Serves 4

Total time: 15 minutes

1½ tbsp olive oil
1½ tbsp white wine vinegar
2 slices white bread, crusts removed
2 green peppers, seeded and chopped
1 cucumber, peeled, seeded and chopped
1½ lb/700g fresh tomatoes, peeled and seeded
1 Spanish onion, peeled and chopped
2 cloves garlic, peeled and chopped
1oz/25g ground almonds
salt and freshly ground black pepper
4 ice cubes
chopped fresh parsley, for decoration

Mix oil and vinegar together, then soak the bread in it. Squeeze bread to remove excess.

Reserve a few pieces of pepper and cucumber for garnish. Liquidise the remaining pieces of pepper and cucumber with the tomatoes, onion, garlic, ground almonds and squeezed-out bread in a food processor or blender. Season to taste. Dilute with cold water but not too much – this soup should have a thickish consistency.

Stir in ice cubes just before serving. Cut the reserved pieces of pepper and cucumber into tiny dice and use to garnish the soup. Sprinkle with parsley.

Michelangelo

—◇—

A rich tasting vegetable soup which is quick, easy and cheap to make.

Serves 4

Total time: 30 minutes

1 tbsp oil
½ Spanish onion, peeled and finely sliced
2 cloves garlic, peeled and crushed
4 large ripe tomatoes, chopped
2 pints/1.1 litres vegetable stock
1 bay leaf
2 sprigs fresh thyme
1lb/450g potatoes, peeled and cut into small chunks
½ green cabbage, shredded
salt and freshly ground black pepper

Heat oil in a deep pan and cook onion and garlic over a gentle heat until soft. Add tomatoes and cook for a further minute.

Pour over vegetable stock and add herbs. Bring to the boil and add potatoes. Simmer, covered, for about 15 minutes.

Add the shredded cabbage, cover and cook for a further 5 minutes or until the potato is tender. Season with salt and plenty of black pepper. Serve with warm crusty bread.

Mia Sicilia
——◇——

A Mediterranean bean stew flavoured with oregano and topped with breadcrumbs, oats and melted cheese.

Serves 4

Total time: 30 minutes

1 tbsp olive oil
1 onion, peeled and finely chopped
1 clove garlic, peeled and crushed
1 large courgette, quartered lengthways and then cut across into chunks
4oz/100g button mushrooms, wiped and quartered
14oz/400g can borlotti beans, drained
2 beefsteak tomatoes, chopped
¼ pint/150 ml vegetable stock
½ tsp dried oregano
salt and freshly ground black pepper

Topping
3 tbsp fresh white breadcrumbs
1 tbsp oats
2oz/50g Cheddar cheese, grated
salt
pinch of paprika

Heat oil and gently fry onion and garlic until soft. Add courgette and cook for a further minute.

Stir in mushrooms, borlotti beans, tomatoes, stock and oregano and season with salt and pepper. Bring to the boil, then reduce the heat and simmer gently for 10 minutes. Pile into a shallow heated serving dish.

Mix breadcrumbs with the oats and cheese and season with salt and paprika. Sprinkle over the bean mix and flash under a pre-heated grill for 3 minutes or until the topping is golden brown and the cheese has melted. Serve with a green salad.

Gardener's Quiche

————◇————

A delicious savoury custard tart filled with fresh vegetables.

Serves 4

Total time: 55 minutes

8oz/225g frozen shortcrust pastry, thawed
1 large cooked potato, peeled, and finely sliced
1 large courgette, thinly sliced
1 tomato, sliced
2 eggs
½ pint/300ml milk
salt and freshly ground black pepper
2 spring onions, trimmed and finely chopped
1oz/25g butter

Lightly grease a 7 inch/18cm flan tin. Roll out pastry on a lightly floured board and use to line the tin. Cover and chill for a minimum of 15 minutes (see page 15). Prick base all over with a fork and line with greaseproof paper. Fill with baking beans and bake blind at 400°F/200°C/Gas 6 for 7 minutes.

Arrange potato slices in a layer on the bottom of the pastry case. Place courgette slices around the edge and fill in the middle with tomato slices.

Beat eggs and milk together and season with salt and pepper. Pour over the vegetables in the flan case. Sprinkle spring onions over the top and dot with butter.

Bake at 400°F/200°C/Gas 6 for 30 minutes or until custard is set.

Great Big Vegetable Pie
———◇———

Loads of fresh or frozen vegetables in a soured cream sauce topped with mashed potato for a fast, tasty and extremely economical dish. Instant mash speeds things up beautifully.

Serves 4

Total time: 30 minutes

8oz/225g frozen baby carrots
8oz/225g cauliflower florets
8oz/225g broccoli florets
2 leeks washed, trimmed and cut into 1 inch/2.5cm lengths
¼ pint/150ml vegetable stock
¼ pint/150ml soured cream or stabilised yogurt (see page 17)
salt and freshly ground black pepper
2oz/50g chopped mixed nuts
2lb/900g mashed potato
1oz/25g Cheddar cheese, grated

Cook carrots, cauliflower and broccoli for 3 minutes in boiling salted water. Drain and put in an ovenproof dish.

Meanwhile, cook leeks in vegetable stock until just tender – about 4 minutes. Remove with a slotted spoon and reserve stock. Put leeks in the dish with other vegetables.

Stir soured cream or yogurt into 2 tablespoons of stock and bring to the boil. Season and pour over the vegetables.

Preheat oven to 400°F/200°C/Gas 6. Beat nuts into the mashed potato. Spoon into a piping bag fitted with a large star nozzle and pipe swirls on top of the vegetables, or spoon on and level with a fork. Sprinkle with cheese and bake until topping is brown and pie is heated through.

Flying Saucers
——◇——

Big flat mushrooms with a cheesy stuffing are served on brown bread croûtons. Serve with a salad for a satisfying main course.

Serves 4

Total time: 12 minutes

4 large flat mushrooms, wiped and trimmed
3 tbsp vegetable stock
salt and freshly ground black pepper
8oz/225g cottage cheese, drained
2oz/50g mature Cheddar cheese, grated
1 tsp Dijon mustard
pinch dried oregano
1oz/25g butter
1 tbsp oil
1 clove garlic, peeled and crushed
4 slices wholemeal bread, each cut into 2 triangles
sprigs of parsley, to decorate

Lay mushrooms in a shallow flameproof dish. Sprinkle over stock and season with salt and freshly ground black pepper. Grill under a high heat for 3 minutes.

Mix together cheeses, mustard and oregano and spoon a little on to each mushroom. Grill for a further 3 minutes or until the cheeses have melted and the mushrooms are cooked.

Meanwhile, make the croûtons. Heat butter and oil in a frying pan with the crushed clove of garlic. When hot, remove garlic and fry bread triangles until golden on both sides and crisp. To serve, lay each mushroom on 2 croûtons and decorate with parsley sprigs.

Jungle Trails

———◇———

Courgettes stuffed with a savoury rice and nut mixture.

Serves 4

Total time: 35 minutes

4oz/100g easy-cook brown rice
1½ tsp concentrated vegetable stock
4 courgettes, wiped and halved lengthways
olive oil for brushing
4oz/100g Cheddar cheese
1 tbsp currants
2 tbsp pine nuts
a few mint leaves, shredded
salt and freshly ground black pepper
sprigs of mint and slices of tomato, to decorate

Put rice in a large pan of boiling water with 1 teaspoon of concentrated vegetable stock and simmer for about 20 minutes or until tender. Drain, reserving the rice.

Meanwhile, brush courgettes with oil and place, cut side down, on a baking sheet. Bake at 400°F/200°C/Gas 6 for about 15 minutes or until soft.

Remove courgettes from the oven and carefully scoop out the flesh using a spoon. Chop flesh and mix with the cooked rice, the cheese, currants, nuts and mint. Mix remaining concentrated vegetable stock with 2 tablespoons of boiling water and stir in.

Pile mixture into the hollowed-out courgettes and return the courgettes to the baking tray. Place under a hot grill for 5 minutes or until brown and bubbling. Serve with a side salad.

Tagliatelle with Garlic and Walnuts

———◇———

The walnuts give this dish a distinctive flavour. You could use flaked almonds or chopped cashew nuts if you prefer.

Serves 4

Total time: 15 minutes

12oz/350g tagliatelle
¼ pint/150ml olive oil
2oz/50g unsalted butter
2 cloves garlic, peeled and crushed
4oz/100g walnuts, chopped
1 tbsp chopped fresh parsley
2oz/50g freshly grated Parmesan cheese
salt and freshly ground black pepper
4 tbsp soured cream or yogurt
extra freshly grated Parmesan cheese, to serve (optional)

Cook tagliatelle in plenty of lightly salted boiling water until 'al dente'. Refer to packet instructions for exact cooking time. Drain and return to pan with 1 tablespoon of olive oil and half the butter. Toss through, place in a serving dish and keep warm.

Meanwhile, heat remaining oil and butter in a pan and gently cook garlic and walnuts for two minutes. Remove from heat, stir in parsley and cheese and season with salt and pepper.

Spoon soured cream or yogurt over tagliatelle, and serve with the hot walnut sauce and extra Parmesan cheese, if liked.

149

Avocado, Sweetcorn and Yellow Pepper Salad

———◇———

This main course salad is quite memorable in texture and taste as well as being a delight to the eye.

Serves 4

Total time: 10 minutes

2 ripe but firm avocados
4 tsp lemon juice
3 yellow peppers, seeded and cut into thin rings
12oz/350g sweetcorn kernels
9 spring onions, trimmed and chopped
6 tbsp Herb Vinaigrette (see page 18)

Peel and stone the avocado, then slice the flesh and sprinkle with lemon juice.

Place sweetcorn in a salad bowl and add peppers and spring onions. Place avocado slices on top and pour over vinaigrette.

Singapore Salad

———◇———

Strips of celeriac and chicory with mangetout and beansprouts in an egg and orange dressing, make a delicious main course salad.

Serves 4

Total time: 20 minutes

1 large celeriac, peeled and shredded
juice of a lemon
1 head chicory, finely shredded
4oz/100g mangetout, topped, tailed and blanched
4oz/100g beansprouts

Dressing
2 hardboiled eggs, shelled
1 quantity Orange Vinaigrette (see page 18)
1 tbsp chopped fresh parsley

Sprinkle celeriac with lemon juice and place in a salad bowl with the chicory, mangetout and beansprouts.

To make dressing, separate the egg yolks from the whites. Sieve the yolks and finely chop the whites. Mix sieved yolks with Orange Vinaigrette and stir in chopped whites and parsley. Spoon over salad and toss.

Digs

———◇———

This is a poor man's Waldorf salad, made with peanuts instead of walnuts. It can be served as a main course accompanied with wholemeal bread.

Serves 4

Total time: 10 minutes

1 head celery, washed and cut into thin chunks
2 large Granny Smith apples, cored and chopped
4 tbsp salted peanuts
3 tbsp sultanas
½–¾ pint/300–450ml Soured Cream Dressing (see page 20)

Place celery and apples in a bowl with peanuts and sultanas. Mix together mayonnaise and soured cream or yogurt then stir into the salad. Turn gently to coat.

WEEKEND
ENTERTAINING

———◇———

The weekend ought to be the time when the working cook can wind down, but it is invariably the only time left in which to do any entertaining and pay back all the debts.

Whether entertaining on a small or large scale, one of the most important things to remember is to keep it simple. You'll thank yourself afterwards if you do!

Many of the menus from the Month of Menus chapter are suitable for a dinner party – particularly if you add a starter or dessert as appropriate. The following recipes are extra special and have been included to extend your repertoire. They can be mixed and matched with dishes from the menu and microwave sections. Choose starters and desserts that can be made ahead, like Chicken Liver Pâté on page 153 (which could be bought ready-made if you're really short of time) and Black Coffee Ice Cream or the trifle on pages 163 and 165.

One of the most practical ways to feed a crowd is an all-in-one dish like Chicken Seafood Salad on page 154. People will feel free to help themselves and there's less washing up too.

Chicken Liver Pâté
———◇———

Homemade pâté is so much nicer than bought, and it really doesn't take much time or effort to prepare. The addition of brandy makes it extra special. Chicken Liver Pâté should be pinkish on the inside, so don't overcook the livers.

Serves 10

Total time: 20 minutes plus chilling time
In advance: make this several hours ahead or the day before.

8oz/225g butter, softened
½ Spanish onion, peeled and grated
2 cloves garlic, peeled and crushed
1lb/450g chicken livers, trimmed
1 wine glass brandy
bay leaf and peppercorns, to decorate
a further 2oz/50g butter to seal
crusty French bread or toast, to serve

Melt a little of the butter in a pan and fry the onion and garlic until soft. Remove from the pan and reserve.

Increase heat and fry chicken livers quickly in batches until brown all over. Remove from the pan as soon as they are browned and allow to cool.

Transfer the livers to a blender or food professor with the onion and garlic. Pour the brandy into the pan and scrape up any bits. Pour into the blender or processor and blend until smooth. Whizz in the butter. Transfer to a serving dish and leave to cool.

When cold, melt another 2oz/50g butter and pour over the pâté to seal it. Decorate the top with a bay leaf and a few peppercorns. Chill in the fridge until needed.

Serve with chunks of French bread or hot toast.

Cheese Mousse
———◇———

A light and savoury starter that's rustled up in minutes, and is then left in the fridge overnight to set.

Serves 10

Total time: 10 minutes plus chilling time
In advance: make this the day before.

12oz/350g curd cheese
2 × 10oz/275g cans condensed consommé
4 tbsp soured cream
2 tbsp grated onion
2 tbsp capers, chopped
salt and white pepper
melba toast, to serve

Beat curd cheese until smooth. Add consommé, soured cream, onion, capers and salt and pepper, and mix well to incorporate. Spoon into a glass bowl and chill overnight until set.

Serve with melba toast.

Pernodine

—◇—

Chicken thighs cooked with butter and shallots and flambéed with Pernod make a simple but impressive dinner party dish.

Serves 4

Total time: 45 minutes

2oz/50g butter
4 shallots, peeled and finely chopped
8 chicken thighs
6 tbsp Pernod
½ pint/300ml chicken stock
salt and freshly ground back pepper

Melt butter in a heavy-bottomed pan. Add shallots and fry until soft. Add chicken thighs and brown on all sides.

Pour over Pernod and ignite – standing well back. When the flames have died down, pour over the stock and season with salt and pepper. Cover with a tight fitting lid and cook over a medium heat for 35 minutes, topping up with extra stock if the level of the liquid gets too low.

To serve, transfer chicken joints to a serving dish and spoon over the juices. Accompany with new potatoes or ribbon noodles and Buttered Mangetout with Pine Nuts (see page 97).

Chicken Seafood Salad

————◇————

A cold all-in-one salad which looks and tastes luxurious even though it's not expensive to make. Below are suggested ingredients which can be adapted to suit yourself.

Serves 10

Total time: 30 minutes

1½lb/700g firm white fish fillets
¼ pint/150ml fish stock
2 tbsp olive oil
2 cloves garlic, peeled and finely chopped
½ Spanish onion, peeled and finely chopped
6oz/175g ready-prepared squid rings
5 × 225g cans cooked rice
10 cooked chicken breast fillets, cut into strips
1 red pepper, seeded and cut into rings
1 yellow pepper, seeded and cut into rings
1 tbsp capers
2 tbsp chopped fresh dill
8oz/225g peeled prawns
watercress, to decorate

Dressing
½ pint/300ml sunflower oil
3fl.oz/75ml white wine vinegar
2 tbsp Dijon mustard
salt and freshly ground black pepper
1 tbsp fresh finely chopped parsley

Place fish in a pan and cover with stock. Poach for about 10 minutes or until cooked (depending on the thickness of the fillets). Drain, cool, then flake.

Meanwhile, heat oil in a frying pan and fry the squid with the garlic and onion for 2 minutes. Don't overcook.

Put rice in a large serving bowl and add peppers, capers, dill and prawns. Mix with your hands. Add the chicken, fish, and squid and onion mixture and mix again.

Shake dressing ingredients together in a screw-top jar and pour over the salad. Turn everything over carefully with a large spoon.

Serve in the bowl or turn out on to a large flat platter and decorate with watercress.

Turkey Dianne

---◇---

This delicious dish of turkey breasts rolled in ground almonds is simplicity itself. It can be partly prepared the day before, to the point where it is ready to be cooked. Or it can be cooked in advance and served cold.

Serves 6

Total time: 35 minutes

6oz/175g ground almonds
6 skinless turkey breast fillets
1 tbsp peanut oil
salt and freshly ground black pepper
2 tbsp sunflower oil
lettuce leaves (if served cold), to serve

Preheat the oven to 375°F/190°C/Gas 5.

Spread out the ground almonds on a flat plate. Brush each turkey breast all over with peanut oil, then roll in the ground almonds to coat. Season with salt and pepper and place on a baking tray.

Drizzle a little sunflower oil over each breast and cook for 30 minutes or until golden brown and cooked through.

If serving hot, place in a warmed serving dish and serve with new potatoes and vegetables. If serving cold, allow to cool then chill until needed. Serve arranged on a bed of lettuce leaves with an accompanying salad.

Swiss Fondue

———◇———

One of the best ideas for an informal party for about 8 guests is a fondue party. This is a particularly good wheeze for the busy cook as all you have to do is buy the ingredients, the guests do the rest themselves! You will need a fondue pot with its accompanying spirit stove, however, and as these can be pricey, it's wise to try and borrow one. Alternatively you could use a flameproof casserole dish placed over a spirit burner.

Serve the Fondue with a large mixed green salad.

Serves 8

Total time: 20 minutes

1oz/25g butter
1 large clove of garlic
1lb/450g Gruyère cheese
1lb/450g Emmental cheese
1 pint/600ml dry white wine
salt and freshly ground white pepper
2 tsp cornflour
4 tbsp kirsch
freshly grated nutmeg
2 loaves crusty French bread, cut into cubes

Ask someone to rub the inside of the fondue pot with butter, then with a cut clove of garlic. Someone else should grate the cheese coarsely (in a food processor if you have one).

Put the cheese, wine, salt and pepper into the pot and place the pot over its burner. Give someone a wooden spoon and ask them to stir continuously until the cheese melts.

Meanwhile, ask someone else to mix the cornflour with the kirsch to make a thin paste. Pour this into the melted cheese while the stirrer keeps on stirring until the mixture thickens. Everyone will be drooling by now. Add freshly grated nutmeg and extra salt and pepper, if necessary.

The fondue is now ready to eat. Each guest takes a long-handled fork, spikes a cube of bread on it, twirls it around in the gooey cheese till it's well coated, pushes it off the fondue fork and on to their plate with a dining fork, then eats it.

Pasta Bows with Ham and Olives

Pasta is excellent for mass entertaining – it's cheap, easy to cook and makes little washing up. This is a fast and simple pasta dish with a surprisingly unusual flavour.

Serves 10

Total time: 20 minutes

1¼lb/600g pasta bows
10 thick slices ham, trimmed and cut into cubes
14oz/400g jar stoned black olives
1 pint/600ml soured cream
salt and freshly ground black pepper

Cook pasta bows in plenty of lightly salted boiling water until just 'al dente'. Refer to packet instructions for exact cooking time. Drain and place in a warmed serving dish.

Add ham and olives to pasta and pour over soured cream. Stir to mix and season with salt and pepper. Serve immediately with crusty French bread and a side salad.

159

Tagliatelle with Garlic Sausage and Mushrooms

———◇———

A deliciously rich pasta dish that never fails to impress.

Serves 6

Total time: 15 minutes

1lb/450g green and white tagliatelle
2oz/50g butter
8oz/225g mushrooms, wiped and sliced
10oz/275g cream cheese
8oz/225g garlic sausage, cut into strips
salt and freshly ground black pepper

Cook the pasta in plenty of lightly salted boiling water until just 'al dente'. Refer to packet instructions for exact cooking time.

Meanwhile, melt butter in a saucepan and gently fry the mushrooms. Melt the cream cheese in another saucepan over a low heat.

Drain the pasta and place in a large warmed serving dish. Add the garlic sausage, cooked mushrooms and melted cream cheese and toss together. Season to taste and serve immediately with a refreshing salad such as Chicory Salad with Walnuts and Oranges (see page 160).

Chicory Salad
with Walnuts and Oranges
———◇———

This bitter-sweet salad goes particularly well with a rich or creamy main course dish such as Spaghetti alla Carbonara (see page 129).

Serves 4–6

Total time: 10 minutes

3 heads chicory, washed if necessary
2 oranges, peeled
2oz/50g walnuts, roughly chopped
6 tablespoons Walnut Vinaigrette (see page 18)

Break up the chicory into individual leaves. Tear large leaves in half but leave smaller ones whole. Place in a shallow serving bowl.

Slice oranges thinly and arrange on top of the chicory. Scatter the walnuts on top, then drizzle over the Walnut Vinaigrette.

Tomato,
Red Pepper and Radish Salad

———◇———

A pretty, red side salad of tomatoes, peppers and radishes. Radicchio
leaves are used to edge the salad bowl for extra effect. Cherry
tomatoes look particularly nice and don't need slicing.

Serves 6

Total time: 10 minutes

1lb/450g tomatoes, sliced or cherry tomatoes left whole
2 large red peppers, seeded and cut into rings
1 red onion, peeled and cut into rings
1 bunch radishes, trimmed and sliced
6 tbsp Vinaigrette (see page 18)
1 head of radicchio

Arrange the tomatoes, peppers, onions and radishes in a glass salad
bowl and pour over Vinaigrette. Tuck radicchio leaves attractively
around the edge of the bowl.

Chocolate Creams

———◇———

Luxurious little puds for really special occasions. Make ahead of time
and leave to set in the fridge until needed.

Serves 6

Total time: 20 minutes plus chilling time
In advance: make this several hours ahead or the day before.

12oz/350g plain chocolate, broken into pieces
4 tbsp strong black coffee
1oz/25g unsalted butter, cut into small pieces
¼ pint/150ml double cream, whipped until stiff
4 eggs, separated

Melt chocolate with coffee over a very low heat, stirring all the time.

Add butter and stir until blended into the chocolate mixture. Remove from the heat and allow to cool.

Beat in egg yolks one at a time, then fold in the whipped cream.

Whisk egg whites until stiff and fold into the mixture. Pour into six individual ramekins or wine glasses and chill in the fridge for several hours until set.

Black Coffee Ice Cream
—◇—

A sophisticated iced dessert with a rich and creamy taste. It's very quick to make, but does take quite a time to freeze, which is why the preparation time is so long. Make it in the morning or the night before, to give it time to freeze completely.

Serves 6

Total time: 1 hour 10 minutes plus extra freezing time.
In advance: make this ahead of time.

1oz/25g sugar
3 tbsp cold strong black coffee
2 tbsp rum
¾ pint/450ml double cream
3 egg whites
fan wafers or dessert biscuits, to serve

Dissolve the sugar in the coffee then add the rum.

Whisk the cream in a bowl until soft peaks form, then stir in the sweetened coffee. Transfer to a large freezer-proof container and freeze for one hour.

Whisk egg whites until stiff. Remove container from freezer and stir well. Fold the egg whites into the coffee cream. Return the container to the freezer and leave to freeze completely.

Serve in scoops with fan wafers or dessert biscuits.

Big Dipper

———◇———

A simple help-yourself pud consisting of bought dessert biscuits like cigarillos, ratafias, *lange du chat* and boudoir biscuits and slices of juicy fresh fruit arranged round a sweet creamy cheese dip. Strawberries, oranges and apples are particularly nice served with the dip. Apple and banana slices should be sprinkled with lemon juice to prevent them going brown.

Serves 10

Total time: 10 minutes

1½lb/700g curd cheese
½ pint/300ml double cream, lightly whipped
4 tbsp runny honey
2 tbsp Grand Marnier
glacé fruits and angelica, washed, dried and chopped
toasted hazelnuts chopped for decoration
crystallised violets
a selection of dessert biscuits
a selection of fresh fruits, prepared as necessary then sliced

Beat the curd cheese smooth then stir in the double cream. Add honey, Grand Marnier, glacé fruits and angelica and stir well.

Transfer to a serving bowl and decorate with hazelnuts and crystallised violets. Surround with biscuits and slices of fruit and let everyone help themselves.

Tropical Fruit Salad

———◇———

Greengrocers and supermarkets are full of exotic and colourful tropical fruits. Choose a selection and simply heap them into a large basket with some red apples and bananas. If you prefer, cut the fruit up to make a Tropical Fruit Salad and serve in a glass bowl with pineapple juice and rum poured over.

Green Trifle
with Kiwi Fruit and Figs

——◇——

Trifle is always a popular dish and the delicate shades of green make this a very pretty pudding when served in a glass bowl. Vary the fruit, if you like. Make two of these trifles to serve 10.

Serves 5-6

Total time: 15 minutes plus setting time

6 trifle sponges
Amaretto, Grand Marnier or sherry, for sprinkling
14oz/400g can green figs
3 kiwi fruit, peeled and thinly sliced
1 pint/600ml ready-made thick custard
a few drops green vegetable food colouring
½ pint/300ml double cream
angelica, to decorate
green glacé cherries, to decorate

Break up sponges and arrange in a large glass dish. Sprinkle over sherry or liqueur and leave to soak.

Arrange figs on top. Cut 3 in half and place them against the sides of the glass bowl with their cut sides facing out. Arrange slices of kiwi fruit vertically around the edge of the dish too.

Add a few drops of green colouring to the custard – be careful you don't jog your hand as the more subtle the colour the better. Mix thoroughly then pour the custard over the fruit and leave to set in the fridge.

Whip the cream until stiff and spread over the set custard. Decorate with little strips of angelica and halved green glacé cherries.

Note: Home-made custard is the most delicious but you can make a really 'un-packet flavoured' packet custard by making it very thick and thinning to the desired consistency with double cream.

165

Pears in Red Wine
——◇——

A very smart dessert for a special dinner party. The pears can be served warm, or made ahead of time and served chilled.

Serves 6

Total time: 25 minutes

6 firm even-sized pears, peeled, with stalks left on
juice of a lemon
3oz/75g sugar
1 stick cinnamon
pinch mixed spice
¾ pint/450ml red wine
3 tsp arrowroot, mixed to a smooth paste with a little water
a few flaked almonds, toasted (see page 29)
a few fresh raspberries, to decorate (optional)

Slice a thin layer from the bottom of each pear so they will stand upright when served. Drizzle a little lemon juice over each pear.

Put sugar, cinnamon, mixed spice and wine in a deep pan. Slowly bring to the boil, stirring until the sugar dissolves.

Add pears, reduce the heat, cover and gently poach the fruit until tender.

Drain the pears and place on a warmed serving dish or individual dishes. Stir arrowroot paste into the wine then bring to the boil, stirring until thickened. Pour some wine over each pear and sprinkle with toasted almonds. Decorate the plates with raspberries.

CAKE BOX

◇

'Cakes' is a heading the busy person doesn't often like to find him or herself turning to. However there are occasions when a cake just *has* to be made, and must not under any circumstances come out of a packet. At least it mustn't appear to have spent time on a supermarket shelf.

You'll find all the recipes here ultra quick 'n' easy to prepare – especially if you use non-stick cake tins which don't need lining.

Don't be put off by the 'total time' each recipe takes to make – most of it is baking time, which leaves you free to get on with something else. The quickest cake to prepare and bake must be the Carrot Cake (see page 140) which takes only 10 minutes to cook in the microwave and can be mixed, baked *and* iced with its delicious cream cheese and honey topping in under twenty minutes.

Dark Chocolate Rum Cake
———◇———

Rich, dark, and chocolatey, this is an especially good cake to make when you want to show off. Sandwiched together and decorated with rum and chocolate butter cream, it looks like the work of a trained pâtissier. You can make the buttercream while the cake is baking.

Serves 8

Total time: 1 hour

8oz/225g butter, softened
6oz/150g soft brown sugar
6 tbsp treacle
4 eggs, beaten
6oz/175g self raising flour, sifted
2oz/50g cocoa powder
2 tbsp rum

Rum and chocolate buttercream
12oz/350g icing sugar
2 tbsp cocoa powder
6oz/175g unsalted butter, softened
1 tbsp rum

Decoration
4oz/100g plain chocolate, grated

Pre-heat oven to 350°F/180°C/Gas 4. Grease two 8 inch/20cm round-non-stick cake tins.

Cream together the butter and sugar until light and fluffy, then stir in the treacle. (It's easier to spoon treacle out of the tin if you dip the spoon in boiling water first.)

Gradually incorporate the beaten egg, adding a little flour with each addition. Sift the remaining flour again with the cocoa powder and fold this into the mix with a metal tablespoon.

Divide the mixture between the two cake tins and smooth over the tops. Bake for about 45-50 minutes. Turn out and cool on a wire rack.

When completely cold, sprinkle each half with a tablespoon of rum.

To make the buttercream, sift icing sugar with cocoa powder and beat into butter. Stir in rum. Sandwich the cake halves together with half the icing and use the rest to ice the top and sides of the cake. To decorate, sprinkle grated chocolate in a wide band around the edge of the top of the cake.

Lazy Glazy Cake
———◇———

This is a doddle of a lemon cake with an unusual sweet-sharp lemon Jack Frosting.

Serves 8

Total time: 1 hour 10 minutes

6oz/150g caster sugar
4oz/100g butter
grated zest of a lemon
2 eggs, beaten
6oz/150g self raising flour, sifted with a pinch of salt
¼ pint/150ml milk

Frosting
juice of a large lemon
1½ tbsp caster sugar

Preheat oven to 350°F/180°C/Gas 4. Grease an 8 inch/20cm non-stick cake tin.

Cream the sugar and butter together till light, pale and creamy. Beat in lemon zest. Gradually beat in the eggs, adding a little flour with each addition. Stir in the milk. Fold in remaining flour with a metal spoon.

Pour the mixture into the cake tin and level the surface. Bake for about an hour until risen and brown.

While the cake is baking, mix together the lemon juice and sugar for the frosting.

Remove the cake from the oven and immediately pour over the sugary lemon juice. The aroma is amazing! Leave to cool in the tin.

Running Shorts Cake

———◇———

This one never fails. It's easily and quickly mixed in one bowl and tastes good, too. The easiest filling is a dollop from the nearest jar of jam, or use whipped cream.

Serves 6

Total time: 30 minutes

4oz/100g self raising flour
1 tsp baking powder
4oz/100g caster sugar
4oz/100g butter, softened or soft margarine
2 eggs

Filling and decorating
jam
icing sugar

Preheat oven to 400°F/200°C/Gas 6. Butter two 7 inch/18cm non-stick sandwich tins.

Sift flour and baking powder into a bowl. Add the rest of the ingredients then beat with a wooden spoon or electric whisk until the mixture is smooth. That's it.

Divide mixture between the sandwich tins. Smooth over the tops and bake for 20 minutes, or until risen, brown and firm to the touch. Turn out and cool on a wire rack. When cool, sandwich the two halves together with jam and sift icing sugar over the top.

Palmiers

———◇———

Palmiers are featherlight and sugary puff pastry horseshoes. The secret of success is in the folding.

Makes 20

Total time: 25 minutes

13oz/375g packet frozen puff pastry, thawed
4oz/100g caster sugar

Preheat oven to 400°F/200°C/Gas 6. Grease a large baking tray.

Roll pastry out to a square ¼ inch/0.5cm thick. Sprinkle with about half the caster sugar. Fold two opposite sides to meet at an imaginary line down the middle of the pastry. Press down gently using a rolling pin.

Sprinkle with half the remaining caster sugar, then fold the long sides to the middle again, as before. You now have a thin oblong. Sprinkle with half the remaining sugar. Next fold one long side over to meet the other long side. You now have what looks like a rolled-up newspaper. Press down gently along the length with a rolling pin to stop it unravelling. Sprinkle on the remaining sugar.

Using a sharp knife, cut the pastry across into ½ inch/1cm slices. Arrange on the baking tray, not too close together so they have room to expand. Cook for 15 minutes or until crisp and golden. Transfer to a wire rack to cool. The sticky caramel sets as the palmiers cool – so if they are intent on staying stuck on the tray, put back in the oven for about 10 seconds to soften the caramel.

Butter Shortbread
—◇—

Crisp and buttery — you can't eat just one piece!

Makes 8 pieces

Total time: 50 minutes

4oz/100g butter, softened
2oz/50g caster sugar
1oz/25g ground rice
6oz/150g plain flour

Heat oven to 325°F/160°C/Gas 3. Butter a 7 inch/18cm sandwich tin.
   Cream butter and sugar together until pale and fluffy. Stir in the ground rice, then sift in the flour, stirring gently to make sure it is all incorporated. Quickly work the mixture into a dough and knead lightly until smooth.
   Press into the sandwich tin and mark into 8 segments with a knife. Bake for 40 minutes – or until just colouring. Remove from oven and re-mark the segments. Leave in the tin to cool. When cool, prise gently out of the tin.

Chocolate Refrigerator Cake
—◇—

A lovely, rich no-bake cake. It's so naughty that you only need a sliver. Make it the day before you need it and chill overnight.

Makes 16 pieces

Total time: 8 minutes plus overnight chilling

6oz/150g butter
6oz/150g plain chocolate
1 egg
1oz/25g caster sugar
6oz/150g digestive biscuits, broken into small pieces (see page 80)

Grease a 6 inch/15cm non-stick loose-bottomed cake tin.

Gently melt butter and chocolate together in a pan over a low heat. Meanwhile, beat egg and sugar together in a bowl until light and foamy.

Gradually add the melted butter and chocolate to the egg mixture. Stir in the biscuit pieces. Spoon the mixture into the prepared tin and press down well. Chill overnight in the fridge. Serve cut into slivers.

Cake-Making Tips
———◇———

- With a little forethought, lining non-stick cake tins doesn't have to be time-consuming. Once you've made one circle and strip of greasepoof paper to line a particular cake tin with, you can use it as a template to cut more. Keep a store of ready-made circles and strips for all your cake tins.
- To soften butter, microwave for a few seconds – keeping your eye on it all the time.
- For best results always pre-heat the oven while you are mixing the cake to ensure the correct baking temperature.
- Use lemon curd, honey, chocolate and hazelnut spread or jam as a quick filling to save time spent making icing.
- A fast cake decoration needed? Place a paper doiley on top of the cake and sift over icing sugar. Carefully remove the doiley.
- Fruit cakes and tea-breads are extra nice when topped with a little warmed runny honey and a sprinkling of demerara sugar as soon as they come out of the oven.

INDEX